Lyndsay Green

International Marine Publishing Company
Camden, Maine

Published by International Marine Publishing Company

10   9   8   7   6   5   4   3   2   1

Copyright © 1990 International Marine Publishing Company

Library of Congress Cataloging-in-Publication Data

Green, Lyndsay.
  Babies aboard / Lyndsay Green.
      p.   cm.
  Includes bibliographical references.
    ISBN 0-07-156030-0
    1. Sailboat living. 2. Sailing—Safety measures. 3. Family recreation. I. Title.
GV811.65.G74   1990
797.1'24'0289—dc20   89-49168
                                                            CIP

Questions regarding the content of this book should be addressed to:

International Marine Publishing Company
Division of TAB BOOKS, Inc.
P.O. Box 220
Camden, ME 04843

Design by Maria Szmauz.
Edited by J. R. Babb and Heidi Brugger.
Typeset by Graphic Composition, Athens, GA.
Printed by Fairfield Graphics, Fairfield, PA.
Unless otherwise noted, all photos by Hank Intven or Lyndsay Green.

To Hank,
Lauren and
Andrea.

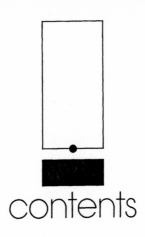

contents

When All Is Said & Done 113

Appendix A

Appendix B

Bibliography

Index 139

acknowledgments

My first acknowledgment must be to the sailing families listed in Appendix A, whose experiences and advice have greatly enriched this book. The amount of time and effort they devoted to telling me their stories reflects both their enjoyment of sailing with their children and their commitment to this project. For this I wish to thank them. Special thanks goes to George and Kathleen Thirsk for their unflagging support.

Several people counseled me, read draft manuscripts, and generally spurred me on. In particular I would like to thank Maureen McEvoy, Susan Oldfield, Janet Rankin-Collie, Ellen Goodman, Jack Horwitz, Hugh Hanson, Margaret Intven, and Laurie Intven. I would also like to thank Susan Main, Patrick Crean, Dennis Deneau, and Allen Stormont for their advice regarding the publishing and distribution of this book. In this regard, it has been a pleasure working with International Marine Publishing, whose professionals are dedicated both to publishing and to sailing. In particular I would wish on all writers an editor of Jim Babb's skill and sensitivity.

This book would not have been possible without the dedication of Ofelia Whitely, who helps take care of our children and does so splendidly. Last but not least, my thanks to my parents, Joan and Stuart Green, and to my husband, Hank Intven, who support me unfailingly in all my endeavors.

introduction

Sometimes, babies end up aboard boats more by accident than by design. Sailing plans often reach the point of no return before baby makes his or her presence known. This was our case. When we took delivery of our first cruising sailboat, a CS 33, I was pregnant and didn't know it. Our first reaction was that if we'd known the baby was on the way we never would have bought the boat. We even considered selling it. You've probably seen these ads:

SAILBOAT FOR SALE - MIRAGE 27 - OUR "BABY" IS FOR SALE BECAUSE A REAL ONE HAS ARRIVED. EXCELLENT CONDITION, NEARLY NEW, MANY EXTRAS. CALL . . . .

Instead, we decided to make the best of "bad" timing. Our elder daughter, Lauren, had her first boat trip when she was six weeks old; by the age of two she had spent a third of her life on a sailboat, including a five-month cruise in the Caribbean. Lauren is now five years old and

"Our times aboard have been some of the happiest of my life, and I'm grateful we didn't pass them up."

teaching the ropes to her two-year-old sister, Andrea. Our times aboard have been some of the happiest of my life, and I'm grateful we didn't pass them up.

Our decision to keep both boat and baby wasn't made any easier by the advice we received. Friends and family were concerned by the perceived risks to our daughter, and our reassurances at the time rang somewhat hollow. We just didn't know enough about what we were getting into, no one we knew had done anything similar, and there were no books to guide us.

This book is the one I wish I had before sailing with our baby. An honest look at both the joys and the difficulties, it provides advice and practical tips for people boating with children under the age of four. In addition, it tells the stories of dozens of other sailing families who have sailed with young ones and survived—even thrived.

In the course of researching this book, I found few people who would change anything about their experiences sailing with young ones, even if they could start all over. Two people said they would have bought a bigger boat, or bought a bigger boat sooner. One family would have bought an outboard motor for their dinghy to ease ferrying the children ashore. Only one person said he would have waited to buy a boat until the children were older. Everyone else was content with the way things happened.

The contributors' recommendations reflect this feeling: Be confident, be positive, and do it. Make sure first that you're a good sailor, prepare adequately, take the proper safety precautions, and go. Don't let your own anxieties or the misgivings of others cause you to miss out.

Some parents won't sail with their children unless everything is perfect; they forget that things are seldom perfect at home. As Margaret Litowich says,

If you are used to sailing as a couple before your first child is born, the baby will change your life on board just as he or she changes your life at home. It helps to be flexible, to have a sense of humor, and to avoid "helpful" outsiders. Since every family is different, not everything that others suggest will work for you.

Laura Estridge agrees:

Don't be afraid. It will be trial and error, with lots of error, but the rewards are worth it. Every boat and every family's expectations are different, but most problems are solved with creativity.

In Leo Litowich's words, "Sailing and kids do mix." We hope that this book will give you the know-how to spend time aboard with your small children in safety and with confidence.

—————•—————
The Contributors

While researching this book I realized how important it would be to reflect a variety of sailing experiences with young children. Every child is unique, boats vary, and every sailing trip is different. To obtain this diversity, I wrote to sailing and boating magazines in Canada and the United States asking readers who had sailed with children under the age of four to fill in a questionnaire detailing their experiences. The response was tremendous, especially given the length of the questionnaire (17 pages). Thirty-five people sent pages of information, often including slides or photographs. Even after deadlines prevented further input, letters kept arriving from sailing parents offering to contribute their experiences to the book.

Many other parents who were thinking about sailing with a baby and had heard about my project wrote with words of encouragement and to ask for a copy of the book as soon as it was available. Several who had trips scheduled already were quite desperate for information and could find little available on the topic.

The contributors are from all over: the Great Lakes and the Pacific and Atlantic Coasts of North America, Ireland, and the Caribbean. Their experience ranges from two weeks on someone else's boat to offshore cruises of several years' duration and full-time liveaboards. I was humbled by their stories, and our minor accomplishment of sailing on the Great Lakes and in the Caribbean—first with one child and now with two—seems tame in comparison.

The Dumaresq family, of Chester, Nova Scotia, sailed along the East Coast for up to three weeks at a time with five children between the ages of 10 and 2. Donald and Patricia Street, from Tortola, British Virgin Islands, started sailing with a baby in 1963; each of their four children sailed from the age of 12 days. The Holdens live aboard in Vancouver with their two children. The elder was eight months old when they went to the South Pacific for two years; their second was born offshore. Pam Achurch singlehanded with a three-year-old son who had been sailing since he was three months old. She did this despite a leg injury that hampered her movements. You'll read more about these people and the other contributors later in this book.

The names of these contributors, and the names of their boats, appear in Appendix A. If you see one of these boats in your travels, you might want to say hello. Unfortunately, I did not get an agreement from any of them to provide babysitting services.

1

making the
decision

What motivates people to take small children sailing? Some people really don't have a choice: Sailing is their lifestyle and the children simply must adapt. Irene Whitney and her husband run Pacific Synergies, a charter boat business that conducts nature and educational sailing trips in the Queen Charlotte Islands and the South Moresby wilderness area off Canada's west coast. Their daughter, born in 1987, has sailed with them on their charters every summer, from the age of six months.

Other people, like Nan and Kevin Jeffrey, have always loved to travel and go on adventures and "a sailboat seemed the best way to continue this lifestyle with twin babies." They began sailing with their twins when the boys were one-year-olds. When the children were two they moved aboard their catamaran and spent the next three years sailing down the Intracoastal Waterway, living aboard in Florida and traveling two winters to the Bahamas.

Others enjoy recreational sailing and don't want to give it up once children arrive. The Hellenbarts were married nine years before having children. By then, sailing had become an important part of their lives: "We wanted to get our children accustomed to a lifestyle that we enjoy." They have sailed Lake St. Clair and the North Channel of Lake Huron with their two children since they were each six weeks old.

These families rejected the traditional alternatives, leaving the children with other family members or baby-sitters while the parents go sailing, in favor of learning to sail *as* a family.

Many parents hope their children's early sailing experiences will result in a life-long love affair with sailing. As Lynn MacDonald explains, "We took our baby sailing because we both love to sail, and we figured it was the most natural thing to do." She hopes their love of sailing will "take root and grow into a real love (of sailing) for our son also."

The Fears

Before their first trip, many people who sail with young children have major reservations about the wisdom of their decision. For some the concerns are always present. These fears stem from a sense of guilt about needlessly endangering your child's safety. After all, most people freely and deliberately choose to go sailing, at least initially, for their own pleasure.

If your child is injured in a car accident, people are unlikely to blame you, nor are you likely to blame yourself, for thoughtlessly exposing your child to the dangers of the road. The car has become an essential and inescapable part of everyday living.

Many of us, however, would find it difficult to cope with the knowledge that our child had been injured because of our desire to go sailing. There is no pat answer to this fear. Although this book will help make your trip as safe and accident-free as possible, each of us ultimately must come to terms with this issue on his or her own.

Pam Achurch, who singlehanded with her three-year-old son, describes her feelings after running aground:

Fortunately, the wind that did come up pivoted the boat and we were able to bounce off just as the Coast Guard came into sight. The "what ifs" of this situation made me throw up out of sheer tension. I felt that I was making choices of putting him [her three year old son] into life and death situations without his consent through my own selfishness . . . Therein lies my dilemma.

By ensuring that people prepare adequately for a trip and remain alert while under way, specific fears actually become useful. The most frequently mentioned nightmare is of the child falling overboard. As Martin Cherry, who sailed with his infant son on Long Island Sound, expresses it, "As for as our experiences, they were all good, except for my own nightmare that Philip went overboard in Block Island Sound."

Young children do fall overboard. But if equipped with life jackets and harnesses they usually suffer nothing more than a scare, and maybe a few bruises. Without proper precautions, however, the results can be fatal. The locals at Nelson's Dockyard in Antigua recall the drowning several years ago of a child who fell overboard. When we arrived there with our toddler we were repeatedly told the horrible story in all its graphic details. Apparently a young child was left attended only by a slightly older sibling; neither wore a life jacket or a harness. Stories like these coupled with our own nightmares remind us to put safety first.

On a minor scale, sailors with small children worry about inconveniencing their sailing partners or marina neighbors. The Litowich family simply spent less time at marinas when their child was an infant, "so that his crying would not bother our neighbors." Others turn this to their advantage. When another boat considers dropping anchor too close to our own, we are not above bringing our two-year-old up on deck to "watch the new boat anchoring." Usually they reconsider. As another sailor put it, "Bringing baby up on deck as we prepare to anchor is the quickest way to clear an anchorage."

Whatever your approach, it should probably include growing a thick skin. Lynn MacDonald found that:

Other sailors shied away from us, never wanting to raft up against us, etc. They didn't want to be bothered by the baby. They thought at first that we were irresponsible, selfish, and just plain crazy. By the end of the cruise we were the talk of the flotilla; we were the "floating nursery," and they could not believe how good the baby was or how easy it was to sail with a baby.

Whatever the concerns and fears, the children who sailed with the families described in this book suffered nothing more than a few bangs and bruises. In fact, it may well be—due to the extra supervision and safety precautions taken by their parents—that they were better off than their "land-bound" counterparts.

The Benefits

For the children. Sailing parents passionately endorse sailing with young children, and feel that children who spend time on boats are better for it. Because they have to learn early on to take responsibility, boat children are more independent and self-reliant. As Patricia Street, whose four children each started sailing at 12 days of age, explains, "They learn to stand on their own two feet at a very early age, to be tolerant and adaptable, and to develop self-confidence."

They also learn about sailing and seamanship. As their skills and knowledge develop, the children gain confidence with boats and on the water. George Thirsk has found, "If the children get good experiences early on, even by age four they will have become good little sailors."

They also must learn to entertain themselves. Having few toys on board means that children must develop their imaginations.

Parents speak also of the advantages young children enjoy when the family is all together in a warm, secure environment. In the close atmosphere aboard boats, children learn to get along well with their siblings. When we asked Andrea at two years of age why she liked sailing, she pointed to each member of her family in turn and said, "Daddy there. Mommy there. LoLo (her older sister Lauren) there. Andy (herself) there." Clearly, the fact that we were all together meant more to her than the specifics of the activity.

On board, fathers often share more of the child rearing responsibilities than they do at home. Sarah Smith and her husband have a daughter who was born halfway through a circumnavigation, in South Africa. They continued back to Florida with their new baby. Sarah appreciated the support and assistance she received from her husband. "That's a nice thing about babies and children on board: The husband/father is always there and gives so much more toward child rearing than in a traditional, land-based family setting."

It's difficult to prove how much toddlers absorb from the different people and lifestyles they encounter as a result of cruising. Parents like to think that this diversity of experience results in children who have more curious and open minds, with highly developed communication skills. In 1984 Linda Starner and her husband took a nine-month, 7,000-mile trip down the Mississippi River and back up the Intracoastal Waterway on a trawler. Their two children were four years and 14 months of age when they

Lauren making friends at Nelson's Dockyard, English Harbour, Antigua.

left. Linda feels that "being exposed to so many different situations and people makes the child a well-rounded individual. They learn a lot about history and geography firsthand."

Doris Hellenbart found that sailing taught her two daughters the art of patience, and that this helps them in other situations, such as lengthy car rides. "They learn that you can't get from A to B just like that. They learn to enjoy the experience while they're getting there as much as when they get there."

Parents feel also that children benefit physically from sailing. They're developing muscles when balancing on a rocking boat, and they're out in the fresh air and in a basically healthy outdoor environment. By the age of 10, Sandra Dumaresq's son had been sailing every summer since he was five months old. He says that the benefits for kids are "heeling over, the fresh air, and exploring."

In general, even very young sailing children learn to appreciate many of the things we take for granted in our convenience-centered lives. They learn that water runs out, that food selection is limited, and that hot water heated in a solar shower bag lasts a limited time. These realities provide excellent opportunities to teach both conservation and the sharing of limited resources.

Sailing children also get to experience nature first-hand. They see birds, animals, and sea creatures that stay-at-home children see only in picture books or at the zoo or aquarium. Our children had the excitement of seeing at very close range a "teddy bear," a small black bear cub swimming across a river in the North Channel of Lake Huron. We came upon it in our dinghy and tried not to frighten it, while at the same time we looked anxiously around for its mother. The cub's wet fur was matted close to its body but its head had stayed dry, and its ears looked big and fluffy for a little bear. It shook itself, bounded up some rocks, and turned to give us a last look before heading into the woods. When we asked our children where the cub was going our two-year-old assured us that it was going to find its mother.

We hope that through living closely with nature our children will appreciate both its beauty and its fragility. If the small sailors of today become the environmentalists of tomorrow we all will benefit.

For parents. One of the great benefits of having young children aboard on trips to new places is that they are consummate ambassadors for their parents. Their smiles

*Experiencing nature, and the foodchain, first hand.
Note that the dodger provides shade from the harsh
Caribbean sun.*

usually open the hearts of the most tourist-hardened local souls. Children are wonderful ice-breakers in situations where language and customs pose barriers. Nothing can bridge national or cultural differences faster than parents chatting together about the universal joys and trials of child rearing, unless it is toddlers eager to make new friends.

Having children aboard can help closer to home as well. Ernie Derushie, who sailed with two children under the age of three on Lake Ontario, finds that having children along makes one more approachable and others more considerate: "People tend to be more accommodating when there are kids aboard; i.e., dock space in proximity to washrooms, finger dock instead of usual bow mooring, etc."

Lynn MacDonald also found advantages to having a baby aboard:

When going through any canal or bridge or into marinas, coves, or inlets, anyone around would say, "Oh, my heavens; look, they have a baby on board." They would immediately come over to talk and ask questions. One thing we found is that we were invited into a lot of very nice people's homes for showers, meals, and to do laundry. We were even given cars to do errands when we were laid over for a day or two.

These introductions via one's children can lead to lifelong friendships. While cruising the Intracoastal Waterway, Anne Driver's family met another sailing family with children of the same age and sex. "Without our children to introduce us we would have missed out on one of the best friendships we've ever had."

Much of the enjoyment that parents find in sailing with their children simply derives from their general *delight* in their children. Children help you become kids again, to see the world with their kind of joyous wonderment. As Linda Starner says, "Just seeing things through the eyes of a four-year-old can be amusing; just having their beautiful smiling faces on board can brighten the rainiest day."

Parents find that sailing also helps them become better friends with their children. The enforced togetherness aboard boats provides a chance for the whole family to become reacquainted and draw closer. At the end of five months' sailing in the Caribbean I felt that the three members of our family often thought with one head and spoke with one voice.

For the parents, especially stay-at-home parents, sailing can be a welcome chance to share parenting responsibilities with everyone aboard. Duties are dispersed among the crew, and the simple presence of other adults or children can reduce a child's dependence on a parent for entertainment. At a practical level, sailing with your children also reduces the expense of babysitting and the guilt felt at leaving them behind.

For those parents who wish to travel extensively with their children, sailing has certain advantages over other means of travel: You never quite leave home. Children love routines. They love to sleep in the same bed every night, eat in the same chair, and follow a predictable pattern each day. Sailing is one way to travel the world yet take your home with you. Baby spends minimal time adjusting to a new environment every time you reach a new destination. And like the Queen of England, you can prevent digestive upsets by carrying your own water and food to foreign destinations.

And Nan Jeffrey feels that if you plan to travel with your children as they grow older it helps to start them early. "Beginning them as babies lays the groundwork for weaning them from the entertainment devices relied on so heavily ashore: television, neighborhood playgroups, an abundance of toys, etc."

Of course sailing also gets you to parts of the world impossible to reach by any other means. Doris Hellenbart loves the North Channel of Lake Huron—mostly inaccessible except to cruising boats and intrepid canoeists—and feels that sailing is the only to truly experience it. Getting there with her family is worth whatever effort it takes.

A boat also provides a unique environment for parents with physical disabilities. Pam Achurch, who was confined to a cast following a series of foot operations, found that it was easier to cope with her son, both as an infant and as a toddler, on a 25-foot boat than in a house:

Almost all activities on a boat this size can be done from a sitting position. In the house, he was more mobile and I couldn't catch him or carry him for some months. It may sound crazy but the boat worked: We didn't have to walk much, people were around to help, and we had water mobility. (Sure beats watching TV with one leg propped up.) I continue to be a handicapped sailor, finding this sport ideal for my needs.

Stuart Rulka's two daughters have sailed since they were six weeks old. Sailing had particular benefits for this family because it was "an instant cure for our older daughter's colic." Stuart adds, "This might be of interest to parents who are contemplating cruising with an infant and are deterred by the thought of being trapped on board with a screaming monster."

Finally, Martin Cherry reminds us of the joys of nursing an infant on a gently rocking boat at anchor:

We basically kept Philip on the same feeding/sleeping time schedule that he was accustomed to on land. Since I was the one who fed him in the morning (usually 6:00 to 6:30 a.m.), I did so on the boat. It was much nicer on the boat to get up early and see the day begin. I somehow felt that everybody who woke up after 7:30 missed the best part of the morning.

---●---

The Downsides

For the children. Children, whether ashore or aboard, are masters at re-orientating the lives of adults to revolve around them. Thus from baby's point of view sailing is not an ideal lifestyle: His or her every need cannot be immediately gratified. Laura Estridge, who has been sailing with her son since he was eight weeks old, explains: "Their needs and desires are often put on hold during a sail change or careful piloting or when weather conditions get sloppy; but these are temporary." Parents argue that although there are long-term benefits to this approach, for the child there is immediate frustration. The ensuing guilt engendered in the parents needs to be acknowledged.

As children become more mobile the boat becomes restrictive. In the early stages of mobility toddlers resent being held, yet they are too unsteady on their feet to be let loose under some conditions. One of the results, as Barbara Ross points out, is that sailing children have "many more bruises than children raised totally on land."

Another result may be delayed walking. Some children who take their first tentative steps before starting a cruise may find their progress delayed. Others may come to rely on handholds aboard and insist on support on land as well. Jo Schneider and Ron Dwelle have two children who both started sailing early: Anna, their firstborn, at four days of age, and Chase, at three months. Anna lived aboard during the summer she was learning to walk. "She was used to the constant movement, so on shore her walking resembled that of a drunken sailor." Don't worry about these temporary setbacks, however. These children are all walking today, upright and unaided.

As children become more sure-footed and mobile, the boat's scant running room offers little space to let off steam. This problem becomes acute, of course, if they're confined for long periods on extended passages or during adverse weather. Sandra Dumaresq finds one drawback of sailing for the children is a "slight lack of exercise. They have pulled the handrails loose from the cabin roof doing loop-the-loops (somersaults) and tying lines to them."

Many sailing families express concern that children

must go without friends their own age for lengthy stretches. They end up spending too much time with adults and not enough time with other children. This can have a negative effect on the children's behavior, as Barbara Ross found. "Because we spent so much social time around adults my daughter became very spoiled and self-centered. Everyone made a fuss over her. Mondays were almost always impossible since she always wanted to go 'back to the boat.'"

Moreover, when children do make friends they all too often have to leave them behind. Pam Achurch found that "changing friends all the time is hard, even if you're only three." Older children often want to bring their friends sailing with them, but this is not always possible or desirable (see "Playmates," in Chapter 7).

Children sometimes find sailing boring and downright unpleasant, but then so do adults. Bad weather can be particularly hard on children if they have to be in the cabin and are prone to seasickness. Ernie Derushie describes one of those particularly unpleasant times:

We had been on the boat about a week or so and had been motoring all day. Everyone was grumpy. There's no standing headroom in our boat; Nicole [the two-year-old] needed to run around; baby Evan was fussy. UGHH!

Larry Snow sailed with three children four years of age and under. He believes that there are *no* benefits for sailing with small children, only detriments. Taking one child under the age of four sailing is "OK," but "any more than one just spells disaster in frayed nerves and short tempers." He has found that the children suffer from a "lack of things to do, short attention span, and they're fidgety."

Another sailor feels that the increased self-reliance common to children who spend their early years aboard may prove to have its negative aspects. Anne Cudmore's two children had both sailed about 8,000 miles before the age of three. The longest period offshore was a four-week passage from the Canaries to Barbados. She feels that since the children must show discipline at a very early age this "can make them take life quite seriously." Too much self-discipline and not enough freedom may make good deckhands but dull children. Kids need free time—time to be kids. The responsibilities of an early life at sea may rob them a bit of their carefree childhood.

For parents. Probably the number one drawback for adults sailing with children is the need for constant vigilance. Children, especially those under four years old, require continual supervision at home and aboard. This can be very draining on parents, who often remain unaware of the source of the strain.

From the moment you board the boat until you go ashore, you never stop being conscious of your child's safety. Some parents talk about developing a "sixth sense" that alerts them to problems. Max Fletcher and his wife left Maine with their nine-month-old son and spent two years sailing to such places as Panama, the Galapagos, the Marquesas, and Tahiti. He found that "subconsciously we were very tuned-in to where Chris was. If we didn't hear him for a second we'd instinctively take a glance to see where he was."

Many people take turns being in charge of the children—knowing where they are and what they are doing—to relieve the strain of constant vigilance. This sharing of child care between both parents alleviates an important inequity: The parent on duty is often below decks and misses out on many of the sights. "Share care" ensures that no one misses all of what's happening in the outside world.

Whatever the arrangement, it is necessary either to have extra hands readily available, or to develop alternative techniques to contend with emergencies. Sometimes both child and boat need attention at the same time.

Whatever adjectives can be applied to sailing with

young children, relaxing is rarely among them. After a long day on the water there are few quiet sunsets, and you seldom spend your rainy days curled up with a book. Patience can wear thin, and at certain points everyone needs a break. At times like these parents long to socialize with neighbors on other boats; enjoy a fine, leisurely meal; or go out on the town. This usually means finding other boats with children and/or a baby-sitter. Sometimes neither is possible. Max Fletcher found baby-sitters hard to come by:

Normally in cruising you haven't been in a particular harbor long enough to get to know potential baby-sitters ashore. While there are plenty of older people cruising who have raised families, we found that these people— while dear friends to us—really weren't interested in baby-sitting, other than perhaps the occasional "desperate" situation. As in anything, there are trade-offs.

Some people going on shorter trips solve this problem by bringing baby-sitters with them. Liz McCaughey, who sails in Lake Ontario with three children, often takes a 12- to 14-year-old baby-sitter with them for one- to two-week stints. Liz finds that, "You need relief from children now and then. It's a good idea to make contacts with yacht club members. They often can help find some sort of child care."

Child care is an absolute necessity when the boat has to be worked on. Repairs or painting often require the use of toxic paints, solvents, or dangerous tools that make it foolhardy to have children underfoot. At times like these, ask other boating families to lend a hand. Failing this the local LaLeche League or parent support groups may be able to assist in finding playgroups ashore or local baby-sitters.

Those traveling alone with children or on extended offshore passages find that fatigue is a major problem. Anne Cudmore's family has done extended passages of up to four weeks' duration. She found that, "Our biggest problem was lack of sleep. We prefer sailing as a family, but when watches are alternating between only two people, and daytime family life makes for broken naps, we were frequently tired."

Preparation takes more time if you're sailing with children. You have to be particularly well organized if you're sailing in areas where you cannot just run out and pick up things you've forgotten. And trips need to be modified to suit children's needs. Ernie Derushie talks about the adjustments you must make in your sailing habits when children are aboard:

The child's well-being comes first. This means compromise. You can't carry as much sail as you'd like, relax as much as when kids are not aboard, [nor can you] sail as long or as often, or go on the spur of the moment. But parents [ashore] have to make similar adjustments to the rest of their lifestyle.

For Lynn MacDonald this adjustment meant "becoming fair-weather sailors."

Basically the only thing we changed was staying in port if it was really storming. There were a few times we normally would have sailed if the baby had not been on board, but we were not on any specific schedule so we relaxed and changed our usual habits a bit.

Sarah Smith found that the worst part of sailing offshore with an infant was "loneliness and worry."

I didn't have anyone to talk to and to ask questions about child care. I had several excellent books but no firsthand experience or personal references to consult. I needed support and encouragement, but we were 1,000 miles from land!

It is important to keep in mind that variations of the above-mentioned problems also apply to caring for small children ashore. Every living space or environment has its own particular dangers. Exhaustion, loneliness, and worry are not unknown to land-bound parents. And we also have little success finding baby-sitters at home. Responsibility for the well-being of little ones requires adjustments, whether ashore or afloat.

And don't forget that some of the so-called detriments of sailing with small children are in fact ingredients in a recipe for a fuller life. Many a physician, philosopher, and sage has advised us to slow down and smell the roses. Sometimes, as we rush by yet another beautiful spot toward no place truly important, I muse that if our children were with us we would allow ourselves the luxury of lingering awhile.

preparation and safety

General Tips

For the safety of your children and your own peace of mind, I cannot overemphasize the importance of adequate preparation when sailing with small children. It can mean the difference between a fun experience and misery afloat. Keep the following general tips in mind when preparing for sailing trips with young children.

Plan ahead. Take the time to plan your trip carefully. If your children are old enough, get them involved in the preparations. Show your children their life jackets, which are "just like the big kids wear on boats." Let them wear them around the house. Show them pictures of children on board boats, and talk about the things they're going to see and do. Assign them chores, such as picking out three special books to take on the trip.

Take a trial run. If you're planning an extended trip, make sure you can survive a trial run. Even sailors planning a weekend trip might try an afternoon's sail first. If you can arrange it, maximize the chances of success by taking your test sail on a relatively calm, warm, sunny day. That first trip will play a major role in determining how you, your sailing partner, and your children view family sailing. Try not to judge the experience too harshly. The first few times, when everything is new and routines have not been established, are always the hardest. Use these trips to realistically assess whether sailing with small children is for you, and what you need to make it work.

Although we sailed quite a bit with our infant daughter before spending five months in the Caribbean, two trips proved to be particularly valuable practice sessions. We spent one week in the Florida Keys with another family who had a toddler. The toddler's activities gave us a good idea of what our daughter would be like near the end of our own trip. We also spent a weekend on the actual boat that we took to the Caribbean.

We learned a lot from these trips and made one critical discovery: On neither trip did we have a place on the boat where we could leave our child alone in absolute security. For her safety and my sanity I learned that this was essential, and we made some very important modifications to our boat (see page 33).

To reacquaint their children with the boat and to reestablish their sea legs, many seasonal sailors take short trips as soon as their boat goes in the water. The children are then better prepared for longer trips.

Strike a balance. When introducing small children to boating it is very important to strike a balance between warning them realistically of the dangers and terrifying them. If you overemphasize the scary aspects of sailing you may end up with a child who is overly cautious and cannot really relax and enjoy himself. Sue Viano recommends:

Don't instill fear by constantly saying negative things; e.g., "Don't go near the edge, it's dangerous. Be careful you might get hurt."

The editor of this book adds, "We ran into a bit of trouble with our son on this one. Now if anything he's TOO careful."

Plan on short sailing days. Keep the sailing day short and your schedule flexible. This is particularly important if you have a rambunctious toddler. Many people who sail with small children try to sail while the children are sleeping. A good schedule involves setting sail early in the morning and arriving at the anchorage by midafternoon. This allows the small crew some needed shore leave. Given a choice of anchorages, head for the ones with child appeal: beaches, other children, or play areas—at least some of the time.

Barbara Ross planned their trips differently when her family sailed with a baby:

We avoided long hours and long distances; we tried to be accessible to a safe harbor; we avoided night sailing so we could be awake during the day.

Don't set a tight schedule. This is good advice for *any* sailor. It's essential if you have small children aboard. Linda Starner describes the difference:

When you sail with little ones, you alter your plans as needed. Say, for instance, the weather is supposed to change for the worse in the afternoon. If it was all adults, you'd probably try and beat the front, plan on some rough seas and getting wet. With tiny ones on board you must think of their welfare above all else. You just don't take those chances that you would take with capable adults as crew.

Be flexible and try to take things a day at a time. If you relax and adopt a flexible schedule that allows you to anchor early when you come upon a child-perfect beach or to stay put when the weather turns nasty, you'll actually enjoy cruising with children. The slower pace allows you to really savor the trip.

Duplicate home routines. Children love routines. Try to duplicate home routines when planning your trip and equipping your boat. The fewer differences between life at home and life aboard, the easier the adjustment for the child. This includes, for example, retaining bedtime rituals, using the bedding from home with its familiar feel and smell, and bringing along the favorite stuffed animal.

Bring help. For a real holiday for *both* parents, many people suggest that you bring help. Help can take the form of a nanny, baby-sitter, friend, or just an extra pair of hands. It's best if the person has sailed with the family before. At minimum, be sure that you are compatible before setting sail. We all know that sailing trips can test even the closest of friendships. Lesser relationships sometimes don't survive the strain.

I remember friends who arrived in Antigua from the Bahamas swearing that their nanny wasn't going to go a meter further with them. The relationship had so deteriorated that we feared the poor woman would be forced to swim ashore from where the boat was anchored, possessions tied to her back. It is for reasons such as these that many people prefer to sail simply as a family.

If you do sail without extra hands, it's particularly important for the sanity of all concerned that both parents take regular shifts at the helm and share the child care responsibilities.

Be prepared. As a general rule, you cannot over-prepare when you're sailing with children. If you anticipate the worst conditions, then you're ready if they materialize and pleasantly surprised if they don't. As Linda Starner recommends:

If you're headed out to a remote island for a few days, stock up for a month's stay. You never know what can happen to change your plans to return: weather, illness, etc. Plan for the worst.

As part of your preparations make sure that you can handle your boat under all conditions. With children aboard it's even more important than usual to establish procedures to deal with emergencies, such as person overboard, sudden squalls, engine trouble at critical moments, etc. Both partners should be able to singlehand and be familiar with navigation techniques. Each parent should be able to handle the boat alone in the event that the other is disabled or lost overboard.

You should have a plan to deal with those times when all adult hands are required on deck. As part of this plan, create a safe place in the boat where you can leave your children without supervision and be confident that they cannot injure themselves. They may get mad and scream and cry, but they'll be safe.

Know your survival techniques. Familiarize yourself with survival techniques to suit your particular sailing conditions. For example, people sailing in cold water conditions should know the techniques that ensure children survive an immersion. Children's small size and smaller percentage of body fat make them particularly vulnerable to hypothermia. In its brochure, "Cold Water Survival," the Canadian Red Cross recommends the following procedures:

In the event of a family being immersed, it is important for the parents to either get children partially or completely out of the water or on some form of flotation (e.g., an overturned boat). Children should be pulled out of the water first because they lose heat faster than adults. If no flotation is available the adults should sandwich the child or children between them to help equalize the cooling rates of all involved.

Instruct the helmsperson. Helmspersons should inform people below decks of conditions that will change the boat's stability or angle of heel. For instance, when coming about or jibing, or encountering a sudden wake or wave, give a preparatory warning. This allows nursing mothers or children to be repositioned safely.

Store loose items. Keeping the boat shipshape is even more critical when small children are aboard. Loose ropes can be a real hazard to unsteady feet. Keep mooring lines and halyards neatly coiled or store them in ready pouches.

Storing loose items is standard operating procedure when preparing to weigh anchor, but it must be done with extra vigilance when young people are about. Danger can come from the most unexpected sources. Anita and Doug Walter, who lived aboard with their infant son in Vancouver, recount the following close call with an unsecured item:

Christopher's first trip was Easter weekend, when he was two weeks old. Everybody thought we were crazy. Never having hit a rock before, we hit two in one day. The door to our woodstove flew off and fell against the crib on the floor. The door is a piece of heavy solid brass and was very hot at the time. We had a few anxious moments!

Know your child. Some children adapt better to boats than others. Keep your child's strengths and weaknesses, personality and predilections in mind when preparing for your trip. One child may be content to be in a limited space. Another may be more frustrated by the limitations of boat life. But don't make too many assumptions about how your child will react to boating life without firsthand experience. A child who is a going concern on land may calm down aboard. And with the combination of fresh air and the rhythm of the waves, many children sleep more often and for much longer stretches than they do at home.

You might have to modify your boat to respond to a child's particular habits. For example, some children are more curious about mechanical things than others and can't keep their hands off the instrument panel or the engine controls. The Holden family finally built a box to protect the autopilot. They found that the knobs were within their daughter's reach and the dials had to be watched constantly to keep the settings from getting changed by little fingers.

Everyone agrees that infants in arms are particularly well suited to boat life, doing little more than eating and sleeping. Margaret Litowich describes this stage:

Leo J. was born July 9, 1985. During his first sailing season he was an immobile infant, unable to sit up or roll over. He was breast-fed and ate nothing else. All we needed to bring to the boat was a folding bassinet and the supplies for a changing station. He spent most of his time in a front carrier.

Once children become mobile, however, it's a different story. If there is a worst age to sail with young children it is probably the period commonly referred to as the "terrible twos," between approximately 18 and 30 months of age. Children at this age are fiercely determined to do things on their own, but they don't yet have all the requisite skills. Although most of us find this stage challenging wherever we may be, a boat may exacerbate whatever frustrations toddlers have on solid land.

Don't forget the comfort item. Whatever you do, don't leave behind the child's comfort item, whether it's a love-worn teddy bear, a pacifier, or a favorite blanket. Other toys or diversions rarely will compensate for the absence of the cherished possession, and you may find yourself returning to port for a ragged piece of cloth.

Where possible, have duplicates of essentials. Bring along several pacifiers. Cut the security blanket into a couple of pieces. Break in another teddy bear. Falling overboard is a more permanent loss than being left behind.

Plan for parties. Plan for celebrations that will occur during the trip, and pack the essential ingredients. If no birthday or anniversary coincides with the trip, make one up. Our younger daughter celebrated her second birthday aboard in the North Channel of Lake Huron with a party complete with balloons, party hats, noisemakers, and

Plan for onboard celebrations, whatever the pretext.

candles on iced cupcakes. A full moon party, a solstice party—whatever the pretext—parties are enjoyed by all and create both something to anticipate and memories to savor for the rest of the trip.

Stick to your rules. Think about rules for children in advance and stick to them. "While under way, no coming out of the cabin without wearing a life jacket or harness." "No climbing on the lifelines." "No children allowed on the foredeck without supervision." Whatever your rules, be consistent and enforce them with visiting children as well. Make sure that all adults aboard have the same understanding of the rules: Children are quick to exploit a crack in the united front.

Preparing the Boat

Some boats are more amenable to small children than others. Thus, some people recommend buying your boat with the needs of your children in mind. For example, Ernie Derushie lists the features of his current boat (similar to a Tanzer 22) that make it particularly suitable for sailing with small children:

- *It can be singlehanded under any circumstances.*
- *It is very docile, even when left to wallow while reefing in a blow.*
- *The portlights are located at a very good viewing height; Nicole (his two-year-old daughter) can look out while seated on the Vee-berth.*
- *There is a molded seat, centrally located and facing astern, that is perfectly suited to breast-feeding while under way.*
- *All furniture is a good climbing height for a two-year-old. Also, Nicole can climb in and out of the cabin without being helped.*

Nan and Kevin Jeffrey feel that a multihull is the ideal sailing environment for small children and requires few modifications:

We put netting around the foredeck lifelines (the babies' favorite play area, even under sail), and netting along the edge of their double bunk to keep them from rolling out. Otherwise no modifications were needed, primarily because multihulls don't heel. And, while underway, movement and play about the boat is both safe and nondisruptive because a catamaran's motion is so minimal.

Stuart Rulka points out the advantage of removable salon tables that allow a portable playpen to be set up in the main cabin: "They're a great repository for toys, as well as infants in a sloppy sea."

Some people make their boat easier to singlehand by rigging everything back to the cockpit. George Thirsk describes why his family decided to install roller furling:

Easy motion, little or no heeling, huge deck space, and the ability to get where you want to go quickly combine to make a multihull nearly ideal for children. Jeffrey family photo.

When things get nasty, it's a lot nicer to be able to do things from the cockpit, where you can keep the children in view and be able to react quickly when necessary. It's hard for the helmsman to mind the tiller or wheel, navigate, wonder how the person on the bow is doing, and also tend to the children. It's true that a hanked-on sail usually can be changed quickly, but we fought a big genoa for half an hour once, and that changed our minds. We got the furler the next week and we've been happier ever since. For those who want to be "purists," I say save it for when the kids get older; you have plenty of time.

Many people, however, have to make do with the boat they had before baby's arrival. Parents may also charter or go out on friends' boats and thus need to be prepared to modify a variety of boats for children's use.

General childproofing. Go through your boat the way you would your home, at your child's level, looking for danger. Your aim is both to protect your children from the boat and to protect your boat from the children. Pad or make cushions to cover sharp edges that could injure children. Sharp edges can also be rounded off with sandpaper. Cover shore-power electrical outlets with safety covers.

Make sure cupboard latches work. Working latches are often as safe as the childproof handles you install in your home (until your child figures out the trick!). Keep tools and sharp instruments out of harm's way. Ensure that the fire extinguisher and flares are accessible—but not to the children. Stow poisons, medicine, flammables, etc., in locked compartments.

Make sure that little fingers can't turn on the stove. Turn the gas off at the tank, just in case. Ensure that nothing can fall on the child's playing or sleeping areas. Be particularly careful that ropes aren't hanging within children's reach. Can the seacocks be opened by little fingers, resulting in a flooded boat?

Handles secured at kiddie level can assist children in negotiating their way around a heaving boat. Companionways are particularly treacherous for toddlers. Consider handholds for small fingers and, possibly, rubber treads on the steps. Even with these modifications, some parents require that particularly accident-prone children wear safety helmets while aboard.

Pay extra attention to engines. Cover exposed inboard engines. These often are located within a child's easy reach and remain hot enough to burn skin for some time after use. Whirring belts and chains are particularly attractive dangers to small children. Store ignition keys well away from eager hands. It's amazing how quickly keys can be either turned in ignition locks, tossed overboard, or even swallowed.

Lifeline netting. Opinions differ about the value of installing lifeline netting on a boat. Those who recommend its use feel that it is another barrier to a child's falling overboard. It has the added advantage of saving other items, such as favorite dolls, not to mention sails, from being swept over the side. The Holdens live aboard and spent years sailing offshore when their children were small. Their boat is totally enclosed with 2½-foot netting, which is "still as strong as ever, although it's eight years old. Our children are now eight and a half and six and a half and we're still not prepared to take it off." In addition to the lifeline netting, Janis Couvreux installed netting around the mast to create an outdoor playpen.

Those opposed to the use of lifeline netting feel that parents who rely on it will let down their guard. They also feel that the sooner children develop a sense of caution about the foredeck the better. Doris Hellenbart is opposed to the use of netting:

I've seen some boats that look like playpens; one result is that the parents tend not to supervise the kids as closely. There's a false sense of security. Netting, in fact, gives the kids a foothold to help them climb off the boat. And yet you see kids playing on the foredeck with no lines securing them, no harnesses, and no life jackets.

If you use netting, think of it as just one of the many safety measures that you'll be using for your children. Lifeline netting is not a substitute for a life jacket or a harness. Don't let its presence lull you into inattention and carelessness. Also, make sure that you periodically check the netting for signs of weakness. Sun, salt water, and boat movement can rot or loosen netting twine, often imperceptibly.

Dodgers. Some families rig canvas spray dodgers around the cockpit to protect the children from the elements. This also makes it harder for the children to get out on deck. We found that an overhead dodger was essential in the Caribbean to protect both adults and children from the sun. Many use Bimini tops for the same reason.

Safety seat. Devise a safe area where you can leave your child when all hands are required on deck. This might be the same place where the child sleeps or plays (see sections on Play and Sleeping.) Infants needn't be in a gimbaled cradle, but their cradle, car bed, or basket must be wedged or tied firmly to prevent its sliding around when the boat tacks.

A car seat is a favorite safety seat for children aboard. It should be tied or strapped firmly to an immovable object. Stuart Rulka highly recommends using a car seat on board:

For six years our trademark was the two Strolee car seats strapped to our push-pit. Our children would be seated routinely in these any time we entered or left an anchor-

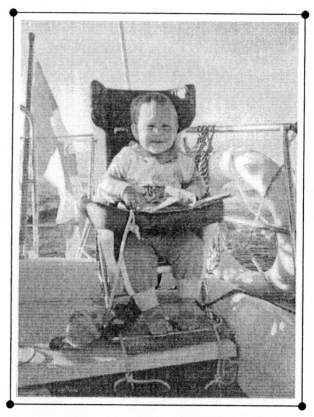

Devise a safe area to leave children when all hands
are required to work ship. This is Kirstie Rulka,
enjoying the best seat in the house. She can be left
more or less unattended, but is free to offer opinions on
your seamanship. Rulka family photo.

age or found ourselves in a situation where both adults
were required on deck. This had the dual benefit of reas-
suring us that they were secure and out of possible harm,
and letting them feel they were involved in what we were
doing. They undoubtedly enjoyed the best seats in the
house!

Because most children are used to car seats from car travel, they may not mind spending long stretches of time in it when on board. Daniel Nichols talks about the other pros and cons of car seats:

Since her car seat can be reclined, Betsy has been known to nap while secured in the seat. We found that we could strap a small tray taken from an old high chair to the horizontal bar in front of the seat. This enabled the car seat to double as a high chair and, as such, solved the significant problem of keeping dining aboard civilized. The car seat is not without its disadvantages, however. The seat is bulky and therefore stows very poorly. It is magnetic, so watch the compass. It also will rust, so keep it below when the rain and spray are flying.

Many people turn their Vee-berth into a childsafe area. We modified a C&C 40 by sewing a canvas barricade for the aft-end of the Vee-berth. It was high enough that our daughter couldn't fall over the top, but low enough that she could peek out and we could peek in. This is where she stayed when all hands were needed on deck. It is also where she napped and played. Other parents rig starboard or port settees with sturdy leecloths or netting.

---●---

Preparing the Child

Swimming. Your children should know how to swim. Some parents teach their children swimming before their first birthday; others wait until two or three years of age. Children should know how to tread water and float on their backs as early as possible.

Some experts such as Whitehead and Curtis—authors of *How to Watersafe Infants and Toddlers*—recommend that you introduce your child to water safety and survival training as early as three months of age. By teaching a child to turn onto his or her back for a breath and to back-float, and to move in the direction of the wall of the pool,

A Vee-berth made childsafe by the addition of a canvas barricade.

grasp the edge, and lift his or her head for a breath, the authors feel that a child who accidently falls into a body of water won't panic and sink. Rescuers will find him or her floating, waiting patiently for help. Your child may even have climbed out of the water unassisted.

Additional skills that Whitehead and Curtis feel a toddler should acquire are blowing bubbles, flutter-kicking with a flutterboard, submerging her face and exhaling underwater, and kick-gliding to a pool's edge.

Finally, even if your young children swim like fish, they are *not* drown-proof. Never leave them unattended while swimming. (For that matter, never leave children under two and a half years old in or near water three inches deep or more. At this age they have yet to develop the reflex that causes humans to hold their breath when their face is submerged.)

Life Jackets. Life jackets (or PFDs: Personal Flotation Devices) should be worn by non-swimmers when they are on or near the water. Non-swimmers aboard boats should always wear a life jacket when on deck. This rule can be difficult for infants to follow, however. We were unable to find a life jacket that fit our daughter properly until she was four months old (she weighed 14 pounds). Prior to that she was rarely on deck unless strapped into her car seat. Her life jacket was always close at hand.

Once your child reaches 20 pounds you should have little difficulty locating a suitable life jacket. Parents are generally satisfied with the quality and comfort of the life jackets available for older small children. Look for these features:

- A through-the-leg strap to keep the jacket from slipping off over the head.
- A comfortable, snug fit.
- A grab handle to ensure speedy retrieval and to which you can attach a security line.
- A flotation collar for head support, to maintain body heat in the water and for splash protection.
- Government safety approval.

Another handy feature is a plastic circle sewn on the back of some makes of life jackets to which you can tie a security line. A tie added to the top of the zipper helps keep little fingers from undoing the jacket. Reflective tape on the jacket shoulders makes the jacket more visible in the water.

The brand name most recommended by contributors to this book was the Mustang Floater. As well as having the essential features described above, its design was praised for being cutaway at the neck. Some other models were found to be uncomfortably tight around the neck.

The essential life jacket. Note the snug fit, through-the-leg strap, and flotation collar with attached grab handle. At four months of age, this life jacket fits fairly well. Smaller life jackets are hard to find, however.

Mustang makes an Infant Floater Vest for children from 20 to 30 pounds and a Child Floater Vest for children from 30 to 60 pounds. Three other recommended brands were Lifeline, U-Vic and Stearns.

How do you get your child to wear a life jacket? Comfort is critical, otherwise wearing the jacket is unpleasant. A good fit is also essential if the jacket is to do its job. Children come in a variety of shapes and sizes, and they keep changing. Even if a jacket fits well one season, it may not the next. Don't solve the problem by buying a vest that the child can "grow into." A vest that is too big is uncomfortable to wear, and more importantly, it may come off over the child's head if he or she lands in the water. The only solution is to keep investing in properly fitting life jackets. Trade with other families as they outgrow theirs.

Parents use a variety of techniques to keep a life jacket on a child, usually combining positive encouragement with simply laying down the law. Sally Holden kept the life jacket in her children's playpen from the time they were very young. That way they "became used to having it around." Sandra Dumaresq found that once children felt that it was "a sign of being a big kid" to wear a life jacket, they wouldn't take it off, not even to nap. Other parents make a big ceremony of taking their child out to purchase the life jacket.

Children should learn that the life jacket is part of sailing, just as the car seat is part of car travel. Many parents have a simple rule: "If you don't want to wear your life jacket, then you have to stay in the cabin." It helps if adults set an example in this regard. It is important for children to see that in rough weather or when sailing at night all hands are wearing life jackets.

Test the life jacket with the child in it, first in the bathtub, then in a pool or at the beach, then finally off the boat. The goal is both to make sure the jacket works and to give your child a chance to feel what it might be like to fall off the boat. This has to be handled carefully, however.

You don't want the child to develop a fear of water and/or the jacket.

Doris Hellenbart threw her daughter into a swimming pool when she was wearing her life jacket. Her daughter was one year old at the time and very at home in the water. Doris recommends the procedure and explains, "I wanted my children to feel comfortable so that if they fell in the water with their life jacket on they wouldn't panic."

While you are testing the life jacket, see how easily you can catch the child using the grab handle attached to the collar. Also test the fit of the safety harness over the jacket.

Some people require that their small children wear life jackets while swimming. It is important to keep in mind, however, that this can hinder a child's learning to swim. Doris Hellenbart found that letting her daughter, who had been taking swimming lessons since she was six months old, wear a life jacket while she was swimming was a big mistake:

She regressed and I had a hard time getting her to swim without a life jacket. Now the rule is that the life jacket is on all the time, except when you're swimming. And adults are always watching while the children are swimming.

Swimmers and non-swimmers alike should know how to swim with a life jacket on, however. They should be able to swim to an overturned object, a rescue aid, or to an outstretched hand. Because a child's body weight is concentrated in the upper part of their body, they do not float easily in a face-up position. The personal flotation device (PFD) is designed to keep them from turning face down once they are face up, but if a child panics, his violent movements could nullify the PFD's effect.

It is essential that small children wear life jackets while on the dock—the site of many child overboard accidents. Children playing with friends can easily walk backwards off the end of the wharf; they may be playing with a toy or fishing rod that falls into the water and instinctively jump in to retrieve it. Too often, these are the times that parents' attention is focused elsewhere. Remember, even when a child is wearing a life jacket there is no substitute for adult supervision.

Harnesses and safety lines. Parents use a variety of methods to attach their child to the boat. Some attach one end of a line to the life jacket and the other end to an immovable object, such as the base of the mast; others have harnesses sewn into the life jacket by a sailmaker. Sometimes, regardless of safety, it is simply too hot for a child to wear a life jacket. When the temperature is at heatstroke level and sailing conditions permit, it makes sense to rely on harnesses alone. The life jacket must be kept within reach, however.

Because of the difficulty of finding commercial harnesses suitable for children, many parents end up having harnesses made to order. Ready-made sailing harnesses usually are made for adults, and even the smallest is often too large. (The harnesses available as walking leashes for children are not suitable for sailing.)

We used a harness made of strapping that was continually getting twisted and bunched up on the skin. The harnesses with solid backs are less complicated to put on and more comfortable to wear. Finding one small enough, however, can be a problem. Two brand names recommended by sailing parents are Lirakis Child's Safety Harness and Jimbuoy. Make sure that the shackle that attaches the harness to the tether cannot easily be undone by little fingers.

As children become old enough to undo tight shackles, they are usually old enough to take more responsibility for their safety. Nan Jeffrey describes this progression:

A harness was worn abovedecks in all situations (sailing or at anchor) until the children were three years of age.

Always have children wear harnesses when on deck. A life jacket may keep an overboard child afloat, but in some sea conditions they can be nearly impossible to find. Cudmore family photo, midway between the Azores and Ireland.

Then, due to their increased dependability, they only clipped them on when underway. By age four the children knew how to clip themselves on or off their line when going above or below decks. The harness lines were permanently clipped amidships to the mast.

Test the harness in a variety of situations. Make sure the tether is not too long: The child could land in the water if he falls overboard or be injured if she falls down the companionway. Laura Estridge's 13-month-old son fell overboard when they were rafted to another boat and he was going from one boat to the other:

He had a harness on and we were two feet away but pre-occupied. As soon as he hit the water the tether was pulled tight, keeping him from going under more than an inch or two. Although initially totally drenched and scared, once into dry clothes he acted as if nothing had happened. For the rest of the vacation, no matter how un-comfortable he was, he wore his life jacket whenever out-side.

In retrospect she feels, "Our attention should not have been allowed to wander, and the length of his tether should have been only 2 to 3 feet (not 5 to 10)."

George Thirsk found that a harness allowed their baby some degree of freedom and gave the adults some peace of mind:

The baby objected to wearing the harness. We handled this by giving him enough scope to travel about, giving him enough things to keep him busy, and keeping in con-tact with him (so he knows you're still there, and didn't leave him tied up!), and finally to catch him when he eventually figures out how to escape from the harness (which will happen by age three at least). The amount of scope we allowed? Let the baby go as far as the edge of the cockpit.

Nan Jeffrey found that sailing a catamaran reduced this problem. "Because a catamaran is so wide, the chil-dren were able to move throughout the boat while teth-ered without any chance of falling overboard."

health

Sailing children are a healthy lot, judging by the experiences of the families who contributed to this book. Their major health concerns were excessive sun exposure and insect bites, both of which are discussed later in this chapter. The only illnesses reported were the occasional cold or high fever and, for one liveaboard family, chicken pox. It is suggested, in fact, that sailing children have fewer colds and other communicable diseases than land-based children because of their reduced contact with people, especially with those great germ carriers—other children.

Medical Preparations

Visit your children's doctor. Consult your children's doctor to determine treatment for common children's medical ailments and stock your first-aid kit and medicine cabinet accordingly. Some useful drugs might require a doctor's prescription. If your trip includes countries with particular health problems, consult a specialist in these regions.

Take first-aid courses. You will be both more knowledgeable and more confident if you take first-aid courses. This should cover the basics of treatment for burns, heart failure, broken bones, and artificial respiration. My Saint John's Ambulance Course came in handy when I had to tie a sling to relieve the strain on my husband's injured elbow, which he received after making an elbow-landing on Nelson's stone quay, in English Harbour, Antigua. Fortunately, our daughters have not required any treatment that would allow me to further hone my skills. Other useful skills one can learn from first-aid courses include how to close lacerations with stitches and how to give injections.

Keep immunizations up-to-date. Make sure your child's immunization program is up-to-date, including tetanus shots, before you set sail. Add other vaccinations recommended by local health offices for your destinations. Make arrangements for necessary shots while you're traveling. Some long-term cruisers bring along disposable syringes so that they can keep up their children's immunization program without medical assistance.

Practice accident prevention. Although it is essential to know how to treat illness and injury, it is smarter to avoid them in the first place. Use common sense and emphasize prevention rather than cure.

Use good medical reference books. Bring along good reference books both for child care and general first aid afloat. My choices are listed in the bibliography in the back of this book.

Know the local conditions. Research the health conditions in the area you'll be sailing, especially if you're traveling far from home. The International Association for Medical Assistance to Travellers (IAMAT; see the bibliography for their address.) publishes useful medical information for those traveling abroad. IAMAT is a nonprofit organization whose services include free booklets recommending immunizations by country, malaria risk charts, and world climate charts.

If you're traveling with an infant, try to find out if there are "well-baby" clinics where you will be traveling, and if there is a charge for their service. You may be able to get immunization shots for your child at the well-baby clinic.

Learn about local hazards. Teach your children not to eat or touch unfamiliar objects: fruit, fish, insects, leaves, etc. For example, avoid the manchineel tree, found in the Caribbean. The fruit is poisonous and the tree produces a milky sap that is a severe irritant to skin and eyes. Even standing under a manchineel tree in the rain can produce symptoms.

Think twice about wading or swimming in fresh water in the tropics because of the dangers of schistosomiasis, a disease spread by freshwater snails. Find out if it is a local problem. (IAMAT publishes a booklet on schistosomiasis.) In addition, find out about local swimming conditions before letting your children go for a swim. Some apparently placid waters may have strong currents or vicious undertows.

Know the local creatures to guard against, whether donkeys, snakes, scorpions, or sea urchins. Remember that your child may be used to friendly domesticated dogs or cats. In many parts of the world cats and dogs are not pets and may be vicious or diseased.

Bring along medical histories. Bring along your child's medical history, including immunization records. This information will be important in case of medical emergency.

●
First-Aid Kit

Step one in stocking a first-aid kit and medicine cabinet is to identify the medical problems your children are most likely to encounter. Then, in consultation with your doctor, work out the appropriate treatment procedures, including medication where necessary. The following alphabetical listing of ailments and medical concerns has been gathered from families sailing in different parts of the world and should be of assistance in your consultations. Add others that may be particular to your child's medical history or to the conditions of the regions you will be visiting.

Some of the medical conditions listed may be more frequent and/or more critical in certain parts of the world; for example infected cuts or insect bites can quickly develop into ulcers in tropical climates. Others, such as malaria, are only of concern in specific affected areas. The length of your trip, the region and country of travel, and the availability of medical assistance will influence the extent of your medical preparation.

Allergic reaction

Bites and stings—from insects, snakes, animals, fish

Bladder infection

Burns, sunburn

Common cold

Constipation

Croup

Cuts

Dehydration

Diarrhea

Diaper rash

Fungal infections

Head injury

High fever

Infections—ear, eye, skin

Lice

Malaria

Muscle soreness

Nasal congestion

Nausea

Pinworm (threadworm)

Poisoning—food, poisonous plants

Pneumonia—viral and bacterial

Roundworm

Sprain

Sunstroke

Teething

Some general tips for stocking the first-aid kit and medicine cabinet:

- Check the expiration date on all medical supplies.
- Discuss potential allergic reactions to medications with your doctor and carry antidotes.
- Carry some prescriptions in powder form to increase their shelf-life and reduce chance of breakage.
- Know the proper dosages relative to age or size.
- Find out which drugs should not be administered together or at the same time.
- Put a note *inside* prescription bottles giving the name of the drug, the dosage, and the use—just in case the labels come off.
- Make sure that you have a rectal thermometer with formulas for conversion from Farenheit to Centrigrade so that you can convey information quickly to medical personnel.

- Carry your own needles and syringes when traveling in foreign countries in case, for example, you require immunization due to an epidemic.

Seasickness

It is widely believed that babies do not get seasick. This may be true for babies, but not for toddlers. The Thirsk's youngest child was prone to seasickness, but only from 16 months to three years of age. As an infant our elder daughter was never seasick, even in the roughest weather. She began to get seasick at the age of 18 months, but even then only under conditions that often made everyone sick: six- to eight-foot swells, beating to windward, etc.

We experienced rough seas during a passage from Martinique to St. Lucia when Lauren was 20 months old. She was sicker than she had ever been, and I felt very badly for her; she really suffered. Small children are resilient, however. Once we got into the lee of St. Lucia she rallied quickly. Two of the adults were similarly afflicted by the passage, but it was many hours before they regained both their good humor and their appetites. Lauren was in great spirits, however, and ate like a horse all night to make up for lost meals.

I always feel very guilty watching my daughters throw up, imagining how wretched they must feel, but the speed of their recovery always consoles me. As soon as we reach quieter waters they are immediately themselves again, and usually ravenously hungry. They also don't seem to hold a grudge against us for having subjected them to such misery. As a toddler, however, when people were talking about sailing, Lauren would sometimes whisper, "Seasick." One time, when I described the color of violet as being "pale purple," she made a gagging motion and said "Seasick," having understood "pail."

Some children, like many adults, including Admiral

Nelson of Trafalgar fame, get sick for the first few hours or days of a long trip before developing their sea legs. Others get sick only on the first trip of every sailing season. Some children in a family may be prone to seasickness, while others may never show symptoms.

If they know conditions will be rough, some parents give their children motion sickness remedies before setting out. (Most such pills can be crushed and diluted with water for administering to children who can't swallow pills.) The medication sometimes makes the children passive and sleepy, and they are able to sleep through the worst stretches. Motion sickness remedies are not always effective, however, and are not recommended for everyone.

The Sun

The sun can be a killer, especially for fair-skinned people and those unused to its strength. When on board, children also are exposed to the sunlight that reflects off the water. The wind that fills your sails dries young skin, making it more prone to sunburn. Small children must be protected carefully from excessive exposure. It is much smarter to prevent sunburn than to rely on medications to treat it. Sunstroke and dehydration must be guarded against.

Children should wear sunscreen and hats. When applying sunscreen pay special attention to the nose, lips, and ears. Another vulnerable area is under and around the eyes. Many sunscreens aren't supposed to be applied near the eyes, but Anne Cudmore found #15 lip shield to be effective for that area.

Hats, as well as keeping sun off heads and out of eyes, can protect sensitive ears from sunburn. Bring several, and allow for growing heads. The hats must have chin straps. Loose 100-percent cotton clothing is recommended, with long sleeves and pants if you have to be out in the tropical sun. Even in more temperate climates children should wear tee shirts when the sun is strong.

Provide a shaded play area by rigging Bimini tops or awnings over the cockpit. We also find a parasol useful to shade our daughters when they are playing in the cockpit

Mad dogs and Englishmen go out in the midday sun. Babies, however, (and the rest of us, actually) should be protected from excessive exposure by parasols—no matter how Victorian one looks. Note that this type of easily stowed front carrier leaves both hands free.

and the sun is hitting the boat at an angle. Try attachable umbrellas that adjust to different angles, such as a golf umbrella. A cheap alternative is a C-clamp lashed to a regular umbrella. Parasols should also be used on the beach and during long walks ashore, especially in the noon-day sun.

Remember to apply sunscreen even if the child is playing under an awning or an umbrella and appears to be out of the sun. Even veiled, the sun's rays can still do damage in the shade.

Sunglasses. Before we left for the Caribbean we had a pair of dark glasses with an ultraviolet (UV) filter made up for our 18-month-old daughter. I knew that she should wear them, but wondered at my chances of getting her to do it. Not only did she get used to wearing her glasses, she would ask for them if she found the sun too bright. We highly recommend dark glasses for little ones who will be spending long hours in the glare of a bright sun. Do not use dark glasses without UV filters, however. By exposing the widened pupil to excessive amounts of ultraviolet rays, they do more harm than good.

The best frames are designed for small children's reading glasses. These have a good deal of elasticity where the arms meet the base, and are quite sturdy. (Our daughter's glasses survived the entire five-month trip.) They must be tied on, of course, and neoprene glasses holders work much better than string.

Insect Bites

The bites or stings of mosquitos, black flies, and other flying insects can pose medical problems for small children. When babies are small their cradles can be completely covered with mosquito netting. As children get older the solutions are not so simple. We found in many

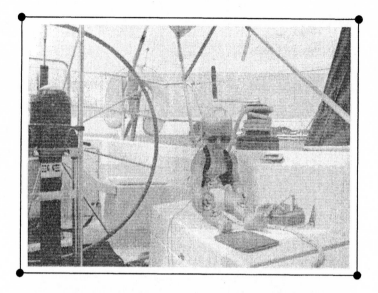

Protect young eyes from the harsh glare of the tropical sun with UV-blocking dark glasses—even when shaded by a dodger or bimini.

locations the only protection was to retire to the boat's cabin after the sun went down and cover all the hatches with mosquito netting.

Parents are understandably reluctant to use insect repellants on baby's sensitive skin. Mounting evidence suggests that DEET, the active ingredient common to most insect repellents, can cause abnormal behavior and irritability—particularly in the young. Some people burn mosquito coils with mixed success. Others try herbal repellents such as pennyroyal oil or Green-Ban. Avon Skin-So-Soft body lotion is mentioned frequently as being very effective against blackflies, and somewhat effective against mosquitos. In truly bad conditions, however, long-sleeve shirts and long pants are often the only answer.

Bites can cause an allergic reaction resulting in swelling, and can become infected if scratched. Ice can reduce both swelling and itching; baking soda can relieve itching. Your first-aid kit should include medication to treat the bites (and antihistamine to counter reaction to scorpion stings and spider bites).

Local Food and Drink

Become knowledgeable about what local food to avoid. For example, eating Caribbean fish that feed off coral may give you ciguatera poisoning. Learn about it before you buy local fish or before you eat what you catch.

Be extremely careful of drinking water. The water that fills your tanks may be unsuitable for drinking—particularly in parts of the Third World. Many people, even those sailing close to home, boil and filter tank water before drinking, or use spring water. Sterilization tablets and filtration cups also can be used.

When going ashore in the Caribbean we always carried drinking water or fruit juices for our daughter because we could never be assured of finding "safe" drinks when we were on land.

If you have a refrigerator, ice cubes are a great amusement and cooler-off for small children. If you have any doubts about the quality of available water, make them from bottled water. Prepare instant baby food or powdered formula with bottled water as well.

Cleanliness

Many techniques are used for keeping small children clean while aboard. When sailing with a baby we brought along a small (30-inch diameter) inflatable infant pool that holds only a couple of inches of water. It was easy to store and a cool place for baby in hot weather. When she was older we used an inflatable pool that just fit the cockpit. It was a wonderful way to keep her cool in the hot Caribbean sun and provided hours of play. These inflatable pools also can serve as playpens when they're empty. (See the section on Swimming in Chapter 2 for cautions regarding "low-water drowning.")

Jo Schneider and Ron Dwelle recommend a Rubbermaid 24-quart "Scrubbin' Tub." "It's good-sized, with plenty of room for a one- to two-year-old to sit in, and it's sturdy." The galley sink is a good size for some children. And don't forget the good old sailing bucket, which works just as well as many of these techniques and has the advantage of being already aboard. Be careful not to leave children unattended, however. The plastic buckets available from restaurants are easy for baby to fall into head-first, but just about impossible for them to get out of.

In some boats you can close the drains in the cockpit or cover the drain holes with duct tape, add several inches of water, and turn the cockpit into a babies' pool. Use a rubber bath mat if the sole of the cockpit is too slippery. Stainless steel fittings in the cockpit, such as scupper strainers, can get hot and should be covered.

Many people use the commercially available sun showers (black plastic bags with a hose and shower head attached that heat water in the sun). The warm-water shower simplifies hair-washing, and serves as a great toy for children who delight in spraying themselves and others. They also allow one to wash off any salt on the skin, which will go a long way towards reducing the chance of salt-water sores and skin infections. Be very careful to test the water first before using it: The sun can heat the water to scalding temperature.

With children aboard, you go through lots of fresh water. And if you run out, it's unlikely that you'll want to repeat the experience. As George Thirsk describes:

Once, with the Sun 27, we ran out of water after a five-day cruise; believe me, it wasn't pleasant aboard until the tank was filled again. Our present boat carries 72 gallons

Plug the cockpit scuppers, add a few inches of water, and you have a secure place for bathing and water play.

in her tanks, plus we cruise with an additional 20 gallons in portable containers, and we have found that isn't really enough, especially with children. This is even more true when you've just found that your toddler has been amusing himself by pumping the Whale faucet in the head. Add extra water capacity to your boat, as it will be money well spent. A lot of boats have water tanks of

The sun shower—a black plastic bag that provides solar-heated water—can provide both for cleanliness and water play. In addition, it's perfect for washing off the salt that accumulates on skin that can lead to skin infections. CAUTION: Check the water temperature before using; it can get HOT.

only 25 gallons capacity. This amount is totally inadequate for cruising with children.

Rain water can be collected and used for washing dishes, clothing, and diapers. One technique recommended frequently is to use your awnings as rain catchers. Sew a hose fitting to a low spot and lead the hose to storage containers.

Diapers

It is fair to say that diapers are the bane of the sailing family's existence. An experienced voice sums it up: "Never sail with anyone who isn't toilet trained." Unfortunately, if you're sailing with babies, you're sailing with diapers.

Disposable diapers are not recommended, because of onboard storage and disposal logistics and because of the broader environmental concerns surrounding them. Storage can be an enormous problem. One family, who crossed the South Atlantic with an infant, needed 18 bags of 30 diapers each to reach the Caribbean from South Africa. "We filled the forward cabin." Most disposables are made, at least in part, of plastic, so that disposing of them at sea is in many cases illegal, and at the very least is morally reprehensible.

Disposable diapers are expensive and, if you are travelling outside North America or Europe, it's a fair guess that they will cost even more than you are used to paying at home. Tourist bureaus in many countries will tell you whether disposable diapers are available and at what price.

Cloth diapers are highly recommended. Because they are washable and reusable, you take fewer of them. Sue Viano found that the number of cloth diapers required for longer trips can be estimated quite accurately:

An experienced sailing friend gave me seven dozen prefolded diapers when she knew we would be long-term sailing with six-month-old Hannah. She said this was the perfect amount—she was right. They were easy to stow when clean, fitted easily into a sailbag, and could be stowed with the sails.

On long offshore trips, and where permissible, you can clean dirty cloth diapers by dragging them astern in an open-mesh bag. You may need to redistribute the diapers in the bag to expose all the soiled areas. Wash them afterwards in salt water and a compatible detergent such as Joy, then rinse lightly in fresh water and fabric softener. If a fresh-water rinse isn't possible (this is a good reason to save rain water), use a liner between the diaper and the baby's skin and apply baby powder liberally. Add disinfectant to the diaper bucket in which you temporarily store dragged but unwashed diapers. Hang diapers on the lifelines to dry; sun-drying disinfects naturally.

Bottom rashes are a realistic concern, but parents report that the instances are rare as long as the child is allowed to go barebottomed for periods of the day and gets exposure to salt air and indirect sun. For persistent rashes, Barbara Ross mixed a diaper cream that combined a small amount of cortisone cream (by prescription) with an antifungal cream (e.g., Microstatin). She found that the fungal-based diaper rashes do not clear up easily when it is hot and humid.

It is important to provide a secure environment for diaper changing. Portable changing pads in pouches are available that can transform the navigation table into a changing table.

Clothing

The general rule about clothing aboard boats is to bring as little as possible. Although easy for adults, this is a bit harder for small children, especially if your trip is a long one. Among other things, small children become larger ones so quickly. It is also difficult if your trip includes different climates. When sailing in cold and damp conditions, for example, it is important to bring extra warm clothes, because wet clothes take a long time to dry. For those days when it's cold sitting in the cockpit and children just cannot seem to get warm enough, a space blanket will do the job.

The Driver family uses a 10-day guide to reduce the amount of clothing needed. Anne Driver's family spent a total of eight months traveling the Intracoastal Waterway south from Baltimore to Clear Lake, Texas. Anne completed the first part of the trip with her husband and two

children, four and two years of age, and then left the boat
to give birth to their third child. When the baby was three
months old she rejoined the boat with all three children
and sailed another couple of months to their destination.
For trips like this Anne recommends:

*Take only about ten days worth of clothes and one good
pair of Velcro sneakers for each child. We have to hit a
grocery store or ice house every three days or so and laundromats have always been available. That info would
have saved me from lugging packing boxes back to the
boat, filling them up with clothes, extra toys, etc., packing
them up for mailing, finding a post office, and spending
another $30 to ship them off to Grandma's!*

If you won't be near stores, however, make sure to
bring duplicates of precious items such as sunhats, shoes,
pacifiers, etc. In fact, three of each essential item is often
needed: one to wear, one that's dirty, and one to change
into.

George Thirsk describes their "backpack system" that
works for a three- to five-day cruise:

*Everyone in our crew comes aboard with their own back-
pack full of clothes (our packs are not large). Everyone
has their own space on board to stow their clothes and
gear. (Do not try to operate out of the packs; they'll be a
mess before the end of one day.) These clothes are "boat
clothes," and are separate from "home clothes," even
though they travel back and forth. When they go home,
they are washed, folded, and immediately repacked for
the next trip. A small amount of backup clothes are always left on board. Don't go to a lot of expense. Just use
extra clothes you generally do not wear much; everyone
has some of those.*

A proper set of foul-weather gear for small children is
very important. None of the sailing families has reported
being able to find small-size sailing gear available com-

It's not that easy to find properly fitting foul-weather gear. Until your child reaches size 2–4, you often must improvise.

mercially, and several people have made their own. Sue Viano made her daughter's oil skins from an old pair of her own foul-weather pants glued together with rubber cement. Zodiac repair glue or any good contact cement should do the trick as well.

Others located adequate raincoats in children's clothing stores. A Swedish company, Abeko, has a line of raingear for children made from polyurethane-coated stretch fabric. It is light, soft, and very flexible. The manufacturers claim that it is tear resistant, mold resistant, and easy to wash. The jacket and pants come in very small sizes, and small hats and overmitts are also available. I have not personally tested this product, but am impressed with the freedom of movement the fabric would appear to permit. For slightly older children (size 2–4 and up), Columbia Sportswear offers its Tadpole Rainsuit (available from REI, P.O. Box 88125, Seattle, WA, 98138), made from PVC-coated nylon.

Proper deck shoes are important for unsteady legs that need all the help they can get. Plastic sandals, such as "jellies," are very useful onshore, and particularly recommended for reef walking, beachcombing, or playing in shallow water. These will protect feet from cuts and scrapes, which often become infected in the tropics.

By 1987, Janis Couvreux had been living aboard and cruising on their 40-foot ketch for six years with two sons, then seven and four years old. Their trips had brought them through Europe, Africa, South America, and the Caribbean, including a 30-day trans-Atlantic passage from Senegal to Rio de Janeiro with an 11-month-old infant. Jan has a great tip for baby messes: "a very compact (two feet wide), European-made electric washing machine (that we plug into a generator)." Those less fortunate will have to rely on the scrub board.

I have included sample packing lists in Appendix B to assist you in thinking through your clothing and other requirements. Obviously these are guidelines only since your particular needs will vary with the age of your children, length of the trip, expected weather conditions, and the availability of laundromats, washing machines, and other supplies.

play

Approach

In many ways a boat is a child's paradise filled with secret hideaways and such fascinating items as winch handles, ropes, and shackles that are ever so much more interesting than conventional toys. Many parents find that their children play better on board than they do at home and are generally more imaginative and inventive. However, the nature of a child's play aboard will vary according to age, energy level, and overall temperament.

Jo Schneider and Ron Dwelle found that the play of their toddler, Anna, is much less structured on the boat. "She seems to get such joy out of very simple things: being in the sun, watching the birds overhead, seeing planes and helicopters, climbing around on the cabintop, peeking in the windows." She didn't pay much attention to the majority of the toys they had with them while living aboard one summer, "yet they took up space and always

A boat is a child's paradise where parents and children often play with the same toys.

seemed to be underfoot. Instead, she enjoyed playing with things already on board, and her father's toolbox never ceased to fascinate her."

Other people find that their children need extra stimulation to keep them happy on long trips. Doris Hellenbart prepares a "goodie bag" for their sailing trips (see page 73). We hide a stash of workbooks and reading books aboard and dole them out during the trip at appropriate intervals. This stream of surprises is definitely more important to our five-year-old than to our two-year-old, however, and the world doesn't end when the supply dries up.

Sailing gives children wonderful opportunities to make their own fun—opportunities that are too often limited in this age of spoon-fed entertainment. Most sailing parents find that their children are able to amuse themselves on board for hours on end with creative play that both incorporates and ignores the boat.

A boat can present particular challenges to a child just mastering playing skills, however. Watching a stack of blocks crash to the ground as the boat pitches, rolls, or heels can be hilarious, but if the blocks can't be stacked

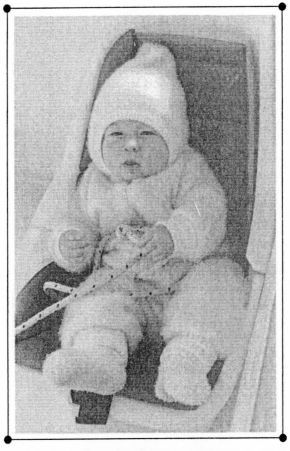

At five months play is pretty basic—often just a bight of line or a shackle.

at all because conditions are choppy, the laughter can turn to tears of rage. As Sally Holden describes:

I recollect how much frustration Roberta had when crossing the Pacific. [Roberta was nine months old when they left Vancouver and two and a half years old when they returned.] In flat seas she could stack her blocks, while the next day the angle of heel would make that impossible. Likewise, one day she could walk, and the next she would have to revert to crawling.

Activities

The following are some play suggestions that have worked for our families aboard.

Going ashore. Despite the joys of sailing, the preferred "sailing" activity of most small children is still going

As is the case with sailors everywhere, shore leave is the preferred activity.

ashore. Shore activities can include gathering items for collections, such as shells, rocks, leaves, flowers, etc. Children can build driftwood forts, look for animals, and play imaginary games. A shovel and pail can keep a toddler amused on the beach for hours.

We store our beach toys in a net bag that keeps the toys accessible but contained and conveniently allows the toys to be rinsed-off and air-dried. Nylon mesh dunk bags made specifically for this purpose are available commercially. For beach outings, remember a change of clothes for the children, drinks and snacks, a sunshade, and skin protection.

Bringing pails filled with treasures back to the boat can extend the shore fun. Tiny crabs, shells, seaweed, and snails are fascinating for little ones to watch and a good primary nature lesson. A dip net is handy for this purpose, and a snorkeling mask can be great fun for children over three. Children form fast attachments to sea creatures. Andrea, at two years of age, was quick to give the appropriate name of "Slimey" to a crayfish carcass and was quite despondent when its stench forced us to dispose of it.

Playing in the dinghy. Playing in the dinghy is another favorite activity. Sandra Dumaresq's children taught themselves to row sitting in the dinghy while it was tethered to the anchored sailboat. By the age of four they could row without being tethered, and as they grew older they used the dinghy as a sailboat. She emphasizes that they have a second dinghy available for retrievals.

Ideally, a dinghy for family use should have high initial stability, positive buoyancy, and perform well under power, oars, or sail. Learning to handle a small boat is an important part of learning to become a sailor, and a dinghy that sails and rows poorly is a difficult handicap to overcome. We use a lapstrake fiberglass sailing dinghy made by Boatex, of Locust Hill, Ontario. Other popular

Learning to row in a tethered dinghy. Thirsk family photo.

designs include Lyle Hess's *Fatty Knees*, the famous Dyer Dhow, *Trinka*, the Halycon Dinghy, and the Spiffy Dink.

Tow toys. Parents report towing toys to be a great source of amusement. The Thirsk's towed a nine-foot inflatable blue whale one summer during all their outings, including a trip from Plymouth, Massachusetts, to New York and back. "It drew all kinds of attention wherever we went." Sue Viano's family tows a sturdy wooden model of a dory behind their boat. Remember that tow lines can easily be forgotten and get caught in the prop. Consider using floating line (polypropylene rope) to reduce the chances of this happening.

Fishing. Fishing, both pretend and real, is a favorite pastime. Children dangle sheets or spare ropes in the water to attract "sharks." At anchor, buckets hung overboard by

A versatile dinghy that performs well under power, oars, or sail can provide hours of enjoyment—not to mention transportation to and from shore.

a rope can also catch "fish." Again, be careful not to let the ropes get wound around the prop. (Use polypropylene rope—which floats—for this as well as for tow toys.) For those tackling real fishing, the simpler the equipment the better. For certain ages a bamboo pole with a hook and bait catches as many fish, with less frustration, than a rod and reel with expensive lures.

George Thirsk highly recommends bringing along fishing gear:

Kids love to fish, even if they don't catch anything. We started out with a drop-line in the shape of a wooden fish and progressed to full-sized rods. Small or folding rods or good drop-lines are probably best. Once while we were at a fuel dock awaiting repairs, instead of letting the kids get bored we let them fish; they caught 12. We were busy just getting them off their hooks into a bucket.

Collecting. The gatherings from shore leave can provide the raw material for wonderful collections. Our elder daughter would play for hours in the cockpit with her shell collection; at 21 months she could distinguish a cowrie from a keyhole limpet. Make or buy simple presses for flowers, leaves, and plants, and devise a simple storage system. Ziploc plastic bags, for instance, can stow small treasures that might otherwise get lost in the bilge and caught in limber holes. Scavenger hunts are great fun and permit organized collecting. Postcard collections also are sources of fun and memories.

Active cabin play. Depending on your level of tolerance and the strength of your cabin interior, active cabin play can be fun. Children can build forts, swing from the grab-rails, and slide down cockpit-cushion slides. Hide-and-go-seek is a favorite activity on board, despite the apparently limited places for concealment.

Plays. Plays and puppet shows are wonderful ways to stimulate your children's imagination and keep them busy at the same time. Bring along grease paint and a few small dress-up props for these times.

Parties. Parties are highly recommended by all parents, especially for extended cruises. In addition to the regular party occasions such as birthdays, anniversaries, national holidays, etc., make any excuse for a party: the first landfall in a few days, baby's first word, the sighting of dolphins—whatever. Be sure to bring along the supplies for such parties and hide them well, to be revealed at the appropriate moments.

Pools. Playing in water, no matter how small the amount, can be immensely amusing for little ones. Use the same techniques that you use to keep children clean: flooding the cockpit, using inflatable pools, pails, and sun showers.

Turning the cockpit into a wading pool by closing the drains is great fun for small children, especially when their older brothers or sisters are swimming off the boat. The little ones feel less left out if they have their own pool, and the adults don't mind having a cool place to soak their feet, either.

Stories, songs, and word games. While under way and seated in the cockpit, keep children amused by telling them stories, singing songs, and playing games like "I Spy." Stories that incorporate recent activities and use elements of nature around them reinforce he child's experiences. Family read-aloud books are popular as well.

Tape recorders. Tape recorders provide fun and comfort. Children can listen to their favorite music or stories from home, record their own sounds and stories, or send messages home to family and friends. Some read-along books come with tapes. Some parents comfort their child with music at times when he must be left alone in the cabin. Music from tape recorders or wind-up music toys often help children sleep at bedtime.

Don't forget to bring extra batteries. Tape recorders are available that can run on 12-volt boat batteries, but the child-operated tape recorders seldom provide this feature. We often bring along both kinds. Extended voyagers can replace the small tape recorder batteries with rechargeable nickle-cadmium batteries (NiCads), which can then be kept charged by small solar-powered chargers, often available for less than $25.00 at Radio Shack.

Books. In addition to bringing books from home, consider making your own. Paste pictures from cut-up magazines, souvenirs, postcards, or stickers onto plain paper, and make up stories together about your trip.

After seeing a goat ashore one day, my daughter and I wrote a story called "Goat on a Boat." In the story, she snuck the goat aboard our boat and the goat got seasick

Forced separation from television make books particularly important on board, and helps foster a life-long reading habit. Cudmore family photo.

(just as my daughter did). Then she showed him all the wonderful things about sailing, including swimming and playing on the beach, and he turned into a fine sailor. We would agree on the words for a page, then during the evening I would draw the accompanying picture and show it to my daughter in the morning. It was a wonderful joint project and a nice souvenir of the trip.

Children's books about boats, harbors, or the sea are popular, both aboard and back at home. As well as being wonderfully entertaining, they reinforce a child's experiences, expand his knowledge and understanding, and refine his boating vocabulary. In the back of this book is a bibliography of sea-centered books that your small children might enjoy. Unfortunately, neither I nor the contributors to this book have been able to locate books *for* small children *about* small children living aboard, with the exception of *Our Home is the Sea*, the story of a boy living aboard his family's houseboat in Hong Kong harbor.

A book of photos from home also can be enjoyable for the child and remind her of friends and relatives. These efforts can backfire, however. We had friends on a one-year cruise who tried to keep memories of home alive by showing their son videotapes of home on their boat's video player. Whenever scenes of his favorite playground were shown, instead of making him happy, he would burst into tears and ask to go home.

Chores. It may seem unusual to list chores as a form of play, but children love to take responsibility. When our children get bored on long passages, our standard ploy is to put them to work scrubbing the cockpit. A pail of water and a scrub brush and sponges keep them busy for hours.

Assigning children chores makes them feel useful and needed and ingrains good habits. They can help do the dishes, wash the floor, participate in baking, and put away their toys. Some families post chore charts, with people's duties changing regularly.

One chore that children particularly love is steering. Barbara Ross finds that their three-year-old loves to hold the tiller and is "almost good enough to keep us on course. It's a great education to show her the compass and get her to try and 'keep the line on the number.'"

Toys

First, two general recommendations about toys: Have a basket, bag, or hammock of toys located in a position easily reached by children. This allows them to pick and choose what they want to play with, when they want.

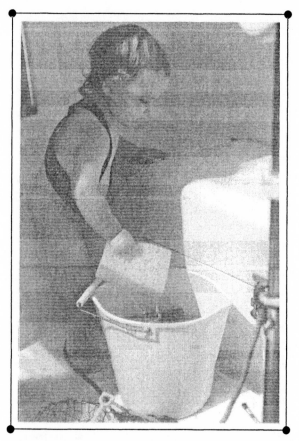

Having baby swab the decks can not only keep her amused, but make her feel part of ship's company.

Second, have what Doris Hellenbart calls "a goodie bag:" a bag of surprises kept concealed from the children. Doris says that their goodie bag is a duffel bag that has changed its contents as the children have grown older:

It contains toys—little things that are new to them, borrowed toys that they'd liked playing with at friends' houses. It was used when things got tough, if I knew we

Steering is probably the most popular "chore" assigned to children of all ages. Cudmore family photo.

were going to be occupied tying up the boat, things were frustrating, or patience was being lost. I would find things from the "goodie bag" that would be appropriate and it always would change their attitude and get them off on a new direction. It's been a salvation to me.

Doris says that the goodie bag is not without its drawbacks: she has to spend the month prior to sailing thinking up new things to put in it, and its contents are becoming more expensive every year as the children grow older and their tastes become more sophisticated.

Careful planning should go into storage places for toys. If possible, the storage spots should be accessible to the children so that they can help in the cleanup. Anne Driver reminds us that it is the small things that drives people nuts and can spoil a trip:

The need for toys and their storage problems can make for cranky, short-tempered adults. It does get rather cramped at times, and stepping on a Lego with your bare feet in the middle of the night on your way to the head can make your teeth hurt.

The ideal toy to have on a boat is one that can get wet without being ruined or leaving stains; one that floats and is small enough to stow; one that is tough and yet won't mark the decks; and, most importantly, one that won't be wept over for days if it goes overboard. What you do not want are toys that are precious, fragile, or would hurt if fallen on. You also have to be careful of tiny toys that can clog the bilge pumps or get caught in drains. Many of the following suggestions come short of this ideal toy on several counts, but they have all been used and appreciated by sailing families.

Infant stimulation toys. Infant stimulation is easily achieved aboard because of the boat's constant motion. Hang mobiles and bells for the baby to listen to and watch.

A clear plastic sphere on a rubber stalk attached by a suction cup can keep baby amused while in the car seat.

Food as play. For young ones, food can be a fun and time-consuming toy that also develops their manual dexterity. Cheerios, raisins, shreds of dry coconut, and popcorn can all be suitable, depending on the age of the child.

Nesting bowls and blocks. Nesting bowls and blocks are as close to the ideal boat toy as you will find. They offer fun both in and out of the pool or bath.

Crayons, paints, and markers. What would childhood be without crayons? Store them in dry lockers, out of the sun, inside plastic tool boxes, Tupperware containers, coffee cans, or Ziploc bags. Big crayons with flat sides reduce rolling. You might want to discard the paper wrappers to

Normally messy markers in use on the "protected"
chart table.

reduce the ensuing mess when they're ripped off by little fingers.

Make sure the paints you select can wash off fiber-glass. Markers usually won't but we used them anyway, under strict supervision. (Washable markers should bead up and wipe off, but may stain.) Be careful, though. Many people have banned markers as being too much of a mess.

Lego or Duplo. These interlocking blocks are a natural for boats: unlike wooden block constructions, they (usually) stay together when the boat moves. Lego pieces are so small that they are always getting lost, but we found the larger Duplo pieces an ideal toy for a one- to two-year-old. As a toddler, our elder daughter built wonderful Duplo constructions that she called "tall things" while under way or at anchor, in the cockpit and in the Vee-berth. We stored the Duplo pieces in a plastic tool box; others reported taking along Legos with success and storing them in a small suitcase.

Playdough. Playdough has both friends and foes; several parents specifically urged that none be brought along. They find that it gets into everything, destroys upholstery, gets stuffed into openings, and can't be removed.

We had good success with homemade playdough when we sailed with only one toddler. Used under close supervision, with our daughter sitting in the top part of a high chair, and kept in an airtight plastic container when not in use, it lasted for months without mishap. We used the dough to recreate some of the highlights of our surroundings: a donkey, the market scene, unfamiliar fruits and vegetables, or people rowing dinghies. Once we had *two* small children aboard, however, supervision became more difficult and playdough was banned from the boat.

Stuffed animals. During our five months in the Caribbean we had a number of small stuffed animals with us that our

COOKED PLAYDOUGH

1 cup flour	1 cup water
1/2 cup salt	1 tablespoon cooking oil
2 teaspoons cream of tartar	food coloring to suit

Put all ingredients in a pot; cook over low to medium heat, stirring, for three to five minutes; knead until smooth and store in an airtight container.

daughter referred to as "The Gang." Great companions and a source of comfort in trying times, The Gang were never allowed on deck unless they, too, were wearing their harnesses (a piece of extra rope tied around them and tethered to a fixed object). Anne Cudmore also found that animals and dolls were great mates for their first son before he had a brother for a friend. A set of stuffed animals lives aboard the Thirsk's boat all sailing season:

If you are on a mooring like we are, it is far easier to have live-aboard stuffed animals than those you would have to ferry in and out by dinghy. The stuffed animals are a comfort when Mom and Dad are busy with the boat, in bad weather, and at night. They're a touch of home. Live-aboard animals should be a number-two comfort item— one they really like but can be away from when they're on land. The number-one comfort item still must travel back and forth.

Some parents don't recommend bringing stuffed animals aboard because they get moldy. It helps if the animals are machine washable and not just surface washable. Others recount their worst sailing moments as those times when favorite animal almost, or was, washed overboard.

Jo Schneider and Ron Dwelle explain the effects of losing Teddy Bear overboard, not once but twice:

***No one allowed on deck without wearing their harness.
That means dolls and stuffed animals, too.***

. . . That had the makings of a tragedy since she [Anna,
their firstborn] can't sleep without him and takes him
everywhere she goes. As it was, we had some tough going
since we had to hang her bear from the boom to dry him
out—which took two days.

Other toy recommendations. Cards, for simple card games, cut-out dolls (some come with magnetic attachments), felt board with felt cutouts, a kite for flying on land and while sailing, bubbles, sewing cards, puzzles, beads on a string, construction material for making your own toys: pipe cleaners, macaroni, paper plates, construction paper, glue, and tape.

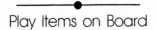

Play Items on Board

A boat holds many items that are not toys but nevertheless have real play appeal for children. The following suggestions have provided hours of enjoyment for small sailing children.

- Ropes. Teach the children to tie knots.
- Winch handles. Let children winch in the lazy sheet on calm days.
- A box of shackles and a pair of pliers.
- A hand-bearing compass. Get a secondhand one if you're nervous.
- Binoculars. If you allow your child to play with your "good" binoculars, put a strap on them and make putting the strap around the neck the first step in the play routine.
- A flashlight. Carry lots of extra batteries (or use Ni-Cads and a small solar charger), and always leave the emergency flashlight untouched.
- Worn-out maps, charts, and parallel rules for charting courses. Let children have their own set to keep in a special place.
- Galley equipment. Bowls, spoons, bottles with tops to put things in, and spice bottles (as long as the tops are firmly attached)—all make great toys.
- A bucket of clothespins.

Mom and Dad "play with them" all day; why not the children? Rope play—even rudimentary knot tying— holds continuous fascination for young sailors.

*A handbearing compass (if it's the only one you have
aboard, supervise closely!) not only may capture baby's
attention, but foster an interest in navigation as well.
Or is that just wishful thinking?*

- A special "tool box" made up for them with keys,
  wires, shackles, etc.
- Fenders. Let children push them around below deck;
  combine them with settee cushions to make forts.
- Folded sails. Use folded sails as horses and set them
  up as slides for toy races.

It should be pointed out that the use of sailing paraphernalia as playthings is not always welcome. Nan Jeffrey describes a few of those times:

*Once or twice we went to release a jib sheet only to find it
elaborately knotted to a number of objects. After that we*

*An extra pair of binoculars (use the neckstrap!) can be
infinitely more amusing than the latest purchase from
Toys 'R' Us.*

*A clamp-on chair attached to the salon table makes a
great place to color. Hellenbart family photo.*

explained a few rules. The babies also had a wonderful
time one day putting Kevin's entire collection of nuts,
bolts, screws, and washers down the hole in the floor
where the table leg goes. We spent hours fishing them out
with a bent coat hanger.

Where To Play

Children play in a variety of locations, depending on their
age. For infants, a favorite technique is to hang them up
in a Jolly Jumper, which can be hung in different locations
in and outside the boat and on land. A hammock also
works well and is a favorite place for older children to
swing on the foredeck.

Judy Button, whose Lazer 28 has a dinette area, recommends that area as a good place to rig a "hanging"
chair for children four years of age and under. "It is re-

A high chair with the legs removed provides a secure place for quieter play that can be moved where necessary around the boat.

strained by shockcords to prevent too much swinging, and a seatbelt keeps our daughter from climbing out. In port, the hanging chair can be removed easily and attached under the boom or in the hatch area."

Another popular swing for the children is made from the bosun's chair, with the degree of swing adjusted by lengths of shockcord according to the child's age (and courage).

Pam Achurch helps her active three-year-old son blow-off steam by letting him swing Tarzan-style on a shockcord curtain rod between the Vee-berth and the main cabin.

The quieter play activities for older small children, i.e., pasting, coloring, etc., often are done at the salon table with a clamp-on chair. We used a highchair with the legs removed, and the tray provided a safe, contained play area for an 18-month-old.

5

eating aboard

Milk

"Breast is best" is the motto of parents of infant sailors. Breast milk has tremendous benefits for children anywhere, but its greatest asset for sailors is its convenience. Breastfeeding avoids the need for sterilized bottles and boiled water, and greatly reduces the chances of the infant getting diarrhea. One major disadvantage, however, is that the father cannot share infant feedings; this may be important on a long passage. For this reason it may be practical to accustom your baby to the occasional bottle. If you prefer to avoid commercially prepared formula, expressed milk lasts 24 to 36 hours in a refrigerator or icebox.

It is also important to carry back-up formula in case of nursing difficulties. Some mothers are prone to seasickness and worry that they might be unable to feed the baby at those times. Also, fatigue and inadequate liquid intake could affect a mother's milk supply. It is important to be secure in the knowledge that formula is available and that baby won't starve.

If your baby has not had formula before, it is safest to choose one for your trip with a soybean base, just in case she is allergic to milk. Cow's milk is one of the principal causes of an allergic reaction during the first year of life. Children may display a wide variety of symptoms including rash, vomiting, and diarrhea.

Commercially prepared formulas are the most acceptable substitute for breast milk in the first six months of life. Formula is digestible, can be absorbed readily by the infant, and includes vitamins and minerals at the approximate levels present in breast milk. Formula also has the proper percentages of protein, fat, and carbohydrates required by a growing infant. Instructions for diluting concentrated and powdered formulas should be followed carefully. Over- or under-dilution of the formula can be dangerous to the child's health.

Unmodified whole cow's milk is not recommended for infant feeding until at least six months of age. Among other reasons, the protein curd is poorly digested and the butterfat is poorly absorbed. Gastrointestinal bleeding may occur if whole milk is consumed in large amounts with little solid food. Whole cow's milk may be introduced once the infant has reached six months and is taking approximately 180 milliliters (12 tablespoons) of solid foods, including iron-fortified infant cereals, vegetables, and fruit.

After being weaned from breast milk or formula, babies need whole milk. Two-percent milk should not be introduced before 12 months of age, and then only if the infant is grossly overweight or not tolerating fat. Partially and totally skimmed milks are too low in total fat and energy content, and are too high in protein and minerals. Totally skimmed milk also cannot provide sufficient quantities of essential fatty acids during the critical first months of life.

Long-shelf-life milk (UHT) is available in many

places, as is powdered whole milk. Also available is vitamin-enriched milk powder, which is more nutritious than skim milk powder. Some families going for shorter trips freeze bags of milk and let them thaw slowly in the icebox. When supplies of fresh milk get low, milk powder can be mixed with the fresh and used for cooking.

----●----
Other Tips

● Plastic bibs with a lip to catch spills cut down on the washing that cloth bibs require, and help keep the boat clean.

● Bring good-quality plastic storage containers of all sizes to store child-size portions of leftovers.

● Bring plastic glasses with lids and straws.

● Bring lots of drinks for children to reduce the chances of dehydration. Fruit juice and sugarless Kool-Aid are recommended. We find small juice boxes perfect for onshore outings, island explorations, dinghy rides, and beach trips. When pre-frozen at home, these also help keep the icebox cool.

● Stock up on foods that are easy to prepare and store. Sarah Smith fed her baby her first solid food offshore and found that strained and mashed winter squash and pumpkins were ideal: tasty, nutritious, and easy to store, with a long shelf life. Her supply lasted three months aboard.

Freeze-dried baby food is easy to cruise with: It's light-weight, comes in unbreakable packaging, and you only mix up as much as you need. For those cruising near home, freeze baby food before leaving in ice-cube trays; thaw the proper portion at mealtime in a double boiler.

● Bring lots of simple finger foods. When your small children are fussy or acting up always consider whether hunger might be the cause. Outdoor activities increase children's appetites; all too often, simple hunger pangs are overlooked in the search for other causes of "bad behavior." We always provision snacks for the children for even the shortest of outings and are inevitably grateful for the foresight.

Where to eat.   A car seat makes a good dining chair for an infant. Sandra Dumaresq also recommends the small

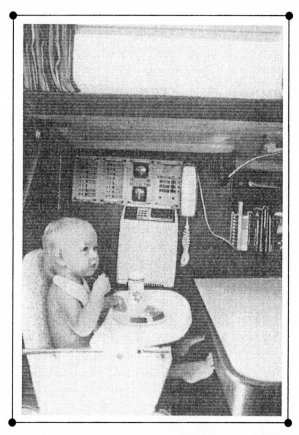

A legless high chair with a tray confines the natural mess of eating, and can be moved where needed around the boat.

terrycloth loungers used for baths, which fold into nothing. For infants who can sit without support, there are a number of chairs on the market that can be clamped onto salon tables. These collapsible chairs are easily stored and also can be carried along for dinners ashore or attached to picnic tables. The table they are secured to must be strong, however.

The clamp-on chair we bought didn't allow our daughter to get close enough to the table; the large gap between table and mouth left a lot of food on the floor. Our solution was to buy an inexpensive metal highchair with a removable tray, and leave off the legs. (Some people with similar problems sawed the legs off old wooden highchairs.) Our daughter also used this seat in the cockpit for playing, coloring, and dough modeling. Its only drawback was that it was bulky to store—a major problem on some boats.

Another idea is to use a wooden or plastic potty chair with detachable tray. These are lightweight and fold up for storage.

Do not serve children food that is too hot. Even at anchor, unexpected motions can flip food into faces or onto laps. Be vigilant when food is cooking on top of the stove for the same reason.

Having spent long periods of time sailing with both our daughters when they were in their "twos," we strongly recommend eating on deck whenever possible. This greatly diminishes the frustration of watching yet another plate hit the deck, if only because it reduces cleaning up after the meal to simply sluicing down the cockpit. Cleanliness is very important in avoiding pesky wildlife that thrive on unclean environments, especially in hot climates.

sleeping

Infants

Infants sleep aboard in all manner of contrivances: canvas hammocks, laundry baskets, car seats, car beds, and modified cradles. We attached a baby's cradle to the boat by lashing it through holes drilled through the teak around the settee.

Patricia Street used a large, rigid, four-handled, handmade Caribbean basket, hung up and thus gimballed, when her four children were infants. When covered, it doubled as a seabag for all the baby's paraphernalia.

Martin Cherry describes the sleeping arrangement he devised for their infant son:

Over the table (amidship), I rigged a straw bassinet supported in the four corners with heavy-duty shockcord run from the hand rails inside the cabin top. In this bassinet he slept and played for hours, constantly being rocked by the motion of the boat. Above his head on the ceiling we

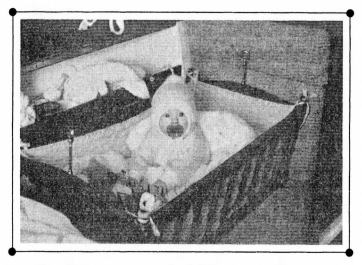

Sleeping arrangements for babies come in all types.
We lashed this standard cradle to the settee.

The Cherry family suspended this bassinet—which had
a built-in rocking motion—from the overhead. Cherry
family photo.

taped pictures and a plastic mirror. The rougher it got, the more he rocked. As he gained weight we had to "anchor" the basket with a line that prevented his swinging too forcibly. We also put up two lines that crisscrossed the top to prevent his being thrown out if a large wake came by.

Margaret Litowich kept their infant in a folding bassinet. When he outgrew this she switched to a Fisher-Price traveling crib/playpen. "The bed was the right size for the settee in the main salon but the legs were not, so we substituted a frame made of plastic pipe. This is where Leo J. slept and where he stood and watched while we were active below decks."

Whatever your system, make sure that the bed is firmly secured and in a location where nothing can fall on it (see story on page 24).

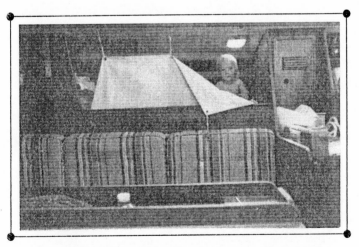

If you're lucky enough to have a boat equipped with the traditional pilot berth, the addition of a lee cloth will make it a secure sleeping area for children.

Toddlers

When children outgrow their baby beds, most people modify boat berths. We modified the Vee-berth in a C&C 40 by making a canvas barrier that closed off the Vee. When guests were using the Vee-berth our daughter slept in the pilot berth. This also was a convenient baby bed because it was rigged with a leecloth that prevented her falling out.

Older boats, like the Street's *Iolaire*—a yawl built in 1905—may have old-fashioned wooden bunkboards.

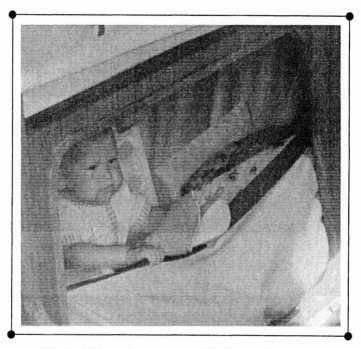

Kirstie Rulka's "house:" a small pilot berth with lee cloth that becomes her own private space for sleeping and playing. Rulka family photo.

These make the berth safe for sleeping at night and suitable as a playpen during the day.

Other families rig up netting or leecloths on the settees. Doris Hellenbart created a safe sleeping and play area in the starboard settee berth of their C&C 35 by sliding the pipe from an auxiliary pipe berth through a net-

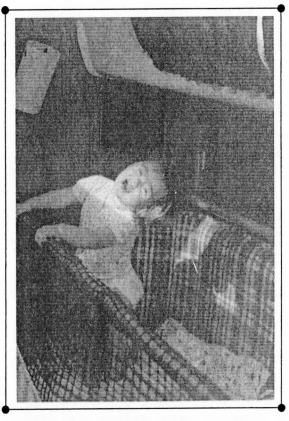

A settee berth made child-proof by the addition of netting suspended from a pipe. Hellenbart family photo.

like curtain material on the top, and fastening the bottom of the material under the settee cushions.

Some people simply bring their playpens aboard and secure them firmly. When devising jury-rigged cribs for infants or toddlers, make sure they conform to crib safety standards; e.g., the child should not be able to get his head stuck between rungs or be in danger of getting caught between mattress and frame.

One consideration in selecting sleeping location is whether the children can leave their beds and go up on deck without your being aware. As George Thirsk explains, "Our children always slept in the Vee-berth. Our theory is that even though we don't get any privacy sleeping in the main cabin, the kids would have to go by us in order to leave the boat. And in the earlier boats, that meant they had to go over us to get out."

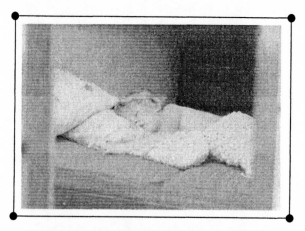

Enclosed Vee-berths can be particularly cozy environments for children. Apart from the myriad nooks and crannies for toy storage with which Vee-berths typically abound, they have an added measure of security: If the kids decide to make a break for it during the night, they first must get by their sleeping parents. Thirsk family photo.

There are several reports of people on watch being startled by the sudden appearance on deck of a small, sleepy figure. Some people rig up tin cans or pots and pans by the companionway ladder to alert them to midnight escape attempts.

Sleeping Techniques

Most people recommend maintaining the same bedtime routines as you do at home. But there are several major differences between home and boat. Depending on the size and construction of your boat and on your sleeping arrangement, you may not be able to say a simple good night and close the child's door. On most boats you're asking your child to fall asleep when you are still plainly visible and quite obviously having a good time—or at least not going to sleep.

As a toddler, our elder daughter found it quite difficult to shut out all this stimulation on her own. Our technique was to turn on some soporific classical music and ask everyone to go on deck or read quietly for the 15 minutes or so that it would take her to fall asleep. The most effectively numbing album we found was Side 2 of Dr. Hajime Murooka's "Lullaby from the Womb" (1974, Toshiba EMI Limited). *Warning:* This music is so sleep-inducing that adults often succumbed before our daughter.

Another favored technique is to turn on the engine at bedtime. The engine's monotonous drone puts many children out like a light. Depending on the condition of your batteries and the availability of shore power, it may be necessary to run the engines at some point during the day, anyway. It may as well be at naptime.

In regions where the sun sets late in the evening, parents find that covering the hatches to block the light makes it easier for the children to fall asleep, and to sleep-in longer in the morning. Hatch covers of sailcloth can be

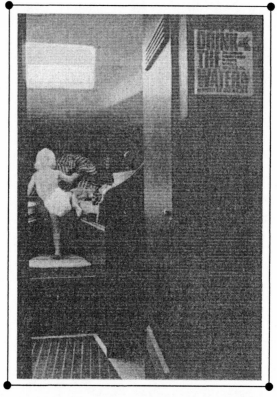

It is important for children to have a private space they can call their own.

made to order, but people use a variety of more primitive techniques, including sail bags and green garbage bags.

Many parents stress the importance of children feeling that they have their own special place on the boat. Stuart Rulka says, "We chose our current boat, a Yamaha 33, at least in part because of its enclosed double pilot-berth arrangement (with standard lee cloths). This provides each child with her own private little castle where she can keep toys and dolls and enjoy a degree of privacy."

Irene Whitney of Pacific Synergies uses a sleeping bag to give her daughter that same sense of possession. As long as she is sleeping in her own sleeping bag, she can "sleep in various berths and feel that she's in her own bed." Moving favorite animals and pictures from berth to berth can help give children a sense of their own space, too.

7

tangential concerns

On Shore

Going ashore to provision with baby in tow is not always easy or enjoyable. Sally Holden says that these were the times she almost regretted having brought baby sailing. "Using public transport, tired, dragging ourselves back to the boat laden with provisions and all the baby gear, trying to get ashore in the dinghy in large surf, trying to leave shore in the dinghy in large surf, often getting swamped," all conspired to cast a shadow over the cruise.

A common recommendation is to indulge in a motor for your dinghy, if you don't already have one. As George Thirsk explains:

If possible, consider a small outboard for your dinghy. With one or more children, the gear you have to haul to the moored mother ship for a decent cruise can sometimes seem tremendous. It will make life a lot easier, es-

An outboard for the dinghy can make the constant coming and going ashore less taxing, particularly for those cruisers who prefer to anchor out. Note the backpack filled with child-support materiel.

pecially in the early years when the kids need an eye (or hand) on them a lot more.

Having a motor-powered dinghy will also make those treks for supplies less onerous, and may mean that you take the children on shore outings more often. We have had trips with small children, both with and without a motor for our dinghy, and now wouldn't be without one.

Unfortunately, each time babies go ashore so goes their gear, making the first order of battle some sort of carrying device: backpacks, strollers, and front carriers, depending on baby's age. We also used a wonderfully simple belt-like shoulder sling for carrying our daughter on hikes.

Backpacks can be multi-purpose. The self-supporting models can be put on the ground for naps and strapped onto a chair for meals. With a zippered diaper bag and a stroller umbrella attached, the onshore family is equipped for many situations. An extra front carrier is useful as a backup in case the backpack gets wet or dirty.

Anne Driver emphasizes the importance of taking strollers on board for each and every child:

. . . That would have saved me a slow trek to town and ultimately an entire day and rental car fee to find the ever-popular but, somehow scarce, umbrella stroller. When not occupied by child they serve wonderfully to carry the 50 pound blocks of ice.

We found another wonderful use for our stroller. On nights when we felt like having dinner in a restaurant we would first put our daughter to sleep in the stroller. We'd then park the stroller in a corner next to our table and enjoy a night on the town, without interruption. Once asleep, even a reggae band with a brass section wouldn't awaken her.

Although strollers and backpacks are a wonderful convenience for parents, remember that they're another source of confinement for your child. Don't be surprised if your toddler would rather tear around the streets burning off cabin fever than sit quietly in some kind of carrying device. Give them some running around time before starting the onshore chores.

Shore packs and diaper bags are essential. Along with diapers, bring along a changing surface (a small towel or extra cloth diaper will do; include plastic bags to dispose of dirty diapers). You should carry a change of clothing, hat, sunscreen, snacks (raisins, crackers), something to drink (juice, water, bottle), and an amusement or two. Don't count on being able to find suitable drinks or food at the moment your baby gets hungry or thirsty. We also found a supply of wet baby wipes invaluable. They were used to clean hands before eating and generally to wipe street dirt off little hands before they went into the mouth.

*Strollers come in handy ashore, carrying children, as
well as ice, groceries, and spare parts.*

One tip offered by Stuart Rulka for trips to the beach
is to keep a bucket of water on dockside (or on deck, if
anchored) to rinse sand off feet. If fresh water can be
spared, so much the better: it can be used to rinse salt off
skin, swimsuits, and towels.

Playmates

Other sailing families are usually eager to raft up. The
children can entertain one another and give the parents
some adult time. George Thirsk says, "When we pull into
a crowded harbor now we scope out the area for another
boat with children aboard and ask if they'd mind a raft.
It's fun, and you get to meet new people."

Barbara Ross's family usually flies an article of children's clothing from the lifelines or flag halyard to attract other children and parents. She thinks it would be a good idea if sailing families flew a burgee signifying "Children On Board." Sue Viano found that their diapers flapping in the breeze eliminated the need for any other special identification; clearly they were a "Boat With Baby Aboard."

Doris Hellenbart enjoys sailing with another couple with children, especially if the children's ages are compatible. Both couples are then provided with more time off. Stuart Rulka agrees. He and his wife bought a boat in partnership with another couple with children, making the total boat crew four adults and four children. The partnership has worked for them but he stresses, "Everyone involved is going to have to be tolerant."

There is a simple rule for having other children visiting on board as guests: Don't overextend the stay. Most children are able to get along for short periods of time, but a boat is a very confined space, and togetherness should not be pushed. If the children are not getting along and you're far from home and shore, you have the makings of a disaster.

The value of having other children visit varies with the ages of all the children involved. Visiting older children can be a real help with minding baby. And extra friends become increasingly important as children grow older. Sandra Dumaresq finds that her children are always better behaved when they have guests. Their family tries to rendezvous with people they know who have children to provide their own with playmates.

Guest children keep your own busy, but they can be difficult if they don't behave or listen. Judy Button suggests that you strictly limit the amount of time that you bring other children sailing with you, unless you have a very big boat. Remember, you must be prepared to watch the visiting children, too.

●

Back Home

Don't be surprised if it takes a while for your children to adjust to dry land after having spent a long time sailing. Many people mention the difficulty their children have sleeping in a stationary bed after the continual movement of the boat. They may also have trouble sleeping in a different room (or bed) from their parents or sibling. Sleeping adjustments can sometimes take several weeks to resolve.

Another problem mentioned frequently is that boat children have no sense of caution regarding traffic. Little people who can work their way around crowded harbors or reeling decks with no mishaps will walk right into the path of a car if not stopped. They have to be watched very carefully until they learn, or relearn, the rules of the road.

Sailing terminology will persist for a long time in a small one's vocabulary. On shore a child's sailing lingo can be both amusing and embarrassing. At two years of age our elder daughter persisted in telling people, to their complete puzzlement, that she "had to go to the head." She would call out "Close the hatches" when it started to rain, whether in a taxi or out visiting. At the age of four, Anne Driver's daughter was watching her grandmother vacuum and called out, "You better let out some more line, Gramma!" You will also notice sailing imagery in small sailors' play, complete with dinghies, lowering of anchors, coming about, and even the occasional running aground.

On a more serious note, we were apprehensive that Lauren at the age of two, after having spent five intensive months sailing with both parents, would have difficulty with life on land where one or both adults were absent for hours at a time. We were both surprised and relieved to find that she went off happily with baby-sitters and to her half-day nursery school with nary a backward glance. Was she relieved to have a break from all that togetherness?

The books tell us that a child's clinginess more often results from too little attention than too much; her easy readjustment seems to bear that out.

Pregnancy

Many women experience no problems sailing when pregnant. The unborn are certainly easy travelers. Judy Button skippered during races when she was nine months pregnant. Sally Holden, however, cautions against long ocean passages early in pregnancy. She had a particularly difficult time during the period between 6 to 12 week's gestation. "I'd never been seasick, hardly any morning sickness, but together . . . !"

Sarah Smith also had problems during this same point in her pregnancy:

I was two months pregnant when we left New Zealand. Two days out we encountered the worst storm in all of our sailing experiences. I was seasick and really worried about a miscarriage. When we reached Australia nine days later, exhausted and with damage to the boat, we thought of shipping the boat home because we had thousands of miles of sailing ahead of us and the Indian Ocean, notorious for bad weather. It's funny how a few weeks of relaxing in a marina can bring on itchy feet. Well rested, boat repaired, and a "go ahead, you're healthy" from a doctor brought us to our senses to keep sailing. We are happy for it.

Sue Viano recounts the story of a pregnant friend who became nauseated by the smell of a particular toilet paper. This side effect was particularly unfortunate under the circumstances since she was sailing from Europe home to the United States, and had fully stocked the boat with toilet paper for the journey.

Do not take medications for seasickness without first

checking with your physician. The packaging on some medications specifically warns against use during pregnancy. And, because the extra water pressure places an additional strain on the heart, scuba diving is not recommended while pregnant.

Margaret Litowich had to miss some sailing time during her pregnancy, and reminds people to keep things in perspective:

We did not sail for six weeks before Leo J. was born because my doctor wanted me to be able to go to a hospital within one hour if necessary. At the time we thought he was wrecking our sailing season. As soon as the baby was born (by emergency C-section), we realized that he was a million times more important than a few weekends on the water. If you plan to sail with your child for 18 years, missing one season during pregnancy is not too inconvenient.

Charters

When chartering a boat it is always important to pay special attention to its seaworthiness. This is even more critical if small children will be aboard. We've seen people whose holidays have been ruined because of charter boats that have been maintained improperly and should have been out of the water a long time ago. You don't want to subject children to these dangers.

Contact charterers in advance to find out if they are sensitive to the needs of sailing families. They may have a boat adapted to the needs of small children or children's gear available for loan.

Racing

People *do* race with babies aboard; they just have to be extra-well prepared and extra cautious. For example, remember to watch carefully when sails are being thrown down hatches; make sure that fast-running sheets or halyards are out of harm's way. And it certainly helps to have additional crew.

Jo Schneider honestly and eloquently describes how tough racing can be when you're short-handed and the crew is limited to baby and her nursing mother:

Racing our boat on Wednesday evenings when Anna was one to two months old was terrible. We were brand new in Newport and knew very few people, so usually we had no crew; occasionally one extra person was on board. Anna usually slept in her cradle carrier until the five minute gun, then would begin screaming. I would go below, nurse her until Ron yelled that he needed me, yank her off, run above to help Ron tack, then go below (all the time trying to balance myself as high up the high side as I could get) to continue nursing our daughter. I learned to despise Wednesdays and would use any excuse to get out of racing.

Judy Button also regretted having brought the baby sailing on their first race in their Laser 28:

It was just my husband and myself with the baby in a 20-knot wind. The boat was heeling so much the baby was rolling in the Vee-berth. This was due to lack of planning on our new boat.

Clearly it becomes easier as the children get older. George and Kathleen Thirsk placed third in a club race with all three children aboard, (ages 4½, 7, and 11 at the time). George says, "Racing with children is not an impossibility for those out there who are interested."

8

when all is said & done

The Bad Times

What moments make you really wonder if you've done the right thing by bringing baby along? What accidents aboard make you feel guilty about subjecting your children to the dangers of sailing?

I am happy to report that most bad times have more to do with discomfort than with real danger. Children get seasick and maybe the parents do, too. People feel miserable and cranky after being cooped up for long stretches. Toddlers get frustrated by pitching and rolling boats while they're trying to learn to walk and find their sea legs at the same time. You get a quiet, foggy day in the marina, perfect for curling up with a good book, but the children can't fall asleep for their afternoon nap unless they're sailing.

George Thirsk describes one of those moments that isn't life-threatening, but nevertheless does make you wonder if it's all worth it:

One of the worst moments was when my wife Kathie was in the galley trying to prepare a meal. We had just come through a couple of line squalls and P.J., the baby, was just **there***, clinging to her leg, not letting go. Of course, this can happen at home, but for some reason it seems worse on the boat.*

First-time parents, especially, report terrible feelings of guilt the first time they have to let baby cry because the sail needs to be changed or the boat docked. All of us who have experienced these feelings know they won't kill you, but you do suffer. It does seem to be a universal experience, however, that parents' hearts have hardened a bit by number two's arrival, and the suffering isn't quite so acute second-time around.

Fortunately, all the accidents reported to me were minor, resulting in nothing worse than bumps, a few stitches in one case, and some good scares—for both parent and child. This finding must be taken as evidence of how careful sailing parents are, rather than as proof that a boat is automatically a childsafe environment.

More accidents are reported from children falling down the companionway or through a hatch than from any other cause. Falls like these have resulted in a tooth through a lip, and in cuts requiring stitches. Other parents have been luckier, and report successful heart-stopping leaps to catch the plummeting body in midair.

Sometimes these falls can be prevented by a shorter tether on the harness. Eric Hatch describes one such incident:

Hilary was an early crawler, and at eight months she lost no time in doing something we thought she couldn't, namely, clamber up the companionway and over the sill into the cockpit. She could also do it in reverse. My first inkling of this came when in the corner of my eye I caught a shape hurtling by, accompanied by a sickening thud and screams. Hilary had chipped a tooth and injured her dignity; her mother was a basket case for hours. We short-ened the tether.

Bumps and bruises can result from falls in other parts of the boat, too, as Jo Schneider recounts:

Newport is not the best protected of harbors, and one day during a gale last August the waves really kicked up. We were preparing to leave the boat for the day when a wave caught the boat just right and Anna was thrown from the port settee into the starboard settee. She ended up with a black eye, a small cut, and bruises on her face. Fortunately she was not badly hurt, but it scared all of us.

The second most reported accident involves toddlers falling overboard, often while the boat is at dock. Fortunately, in each case reported to me the child was wearing a life jacket, harness, or both, and the fall resulted in nothing more than scares all around. Doris Hellenbart recalls the time their 13-month-old daughter fell overboard:

She was kneeling on the bench in the cockpit, pointing at something, and the weight of her life jacket probably continued the momentum. She tumbled into the water. We were motoring in the North Channel, it was June, and the water was very cold. We had a line on her and immediately hauled her up. She was probably only in the water 20 seconds but it really frightened her. For that entire summer, every time we went sailing she would go straight below deck and wouldn't get anywhere near the water. She wouldn't even go swimming. In time it worked itself out.

At 22 months of age our second born, Andrea, fell overboard in similar circumstances in cold June waters at a dock in Georgian Bay. Her older sister was already on the dock, and Andrea could not wait for adult assistance to help her off the boat. She was wearing a life jacket attached by a safety line to the binnacle, and she barely had time to get wet before we hauled her out by the line. She was cold and shocked but the experience did not deter her in the least from sailing, nor seemingly from repeating the performance given the opportunity. I was in much worse shape, however, and took several hours to recover. We were lucky that she fell into the water rather than onto the dock; hitting the dock from that height certainly would have done more permanent damage. It was a good reminder that you cannot be too careful in your attention to safety.

The bad times that are part and parcel of sailing—heavy seas and rough weather—definitely are made worse when little ones are aboard. Linda Starner describes one of these:

Once we were off the Dry Tortugas about 12 miles and got caught in 12- to 15-footers. In a trawler that can be a mighty uncomfortable ride. I was below in the salon holding onto the girls, and Paul was on the bridge looking out for coral heads and markers. We finally decided via walkie-talkies that the situation wasn't going to improve, so we turned around and headed back to the safety of the anchorage and the surrounding reefs of Garden Island and the tiny islands adjacent to it. At that point I was concerned about the safety of the children, thinking that if the boat turtled Paul and I might be able to survive until help arrived, but knowing full well the girls could not. That was one of those times when you say to yourself, "What the heck are we doing?" But then you get to the anchorage, the sun comes out, you clean up the boat, and things don't seem quite so bad. Every hour that passes seems to put things in the proper perspective, and you're ready for another day.

George Thirsk recalled two times when they regretted having small children aboard:

The first time was a trip made in zero visibility fog (our first experience with this much fog) that we made in our

*second year of sailing. While fog has become a way of life
for us now, it wasn't then. We were a bit afraid, yet we
didn't want to pass any of that fear on to the kids. The
second time was this past year in Block Island when a
storm hit—an apparent aftermath of Hurricane Charlie.
We were there for four days and watched 20 to 30 boats
drag anchor and slam down on one another, causing con-
siderable damage and some injuries. We were fortunate
enough to escape any damage, but being trapped on the
boat while all this was going on was a bit scary.*

For us, one of those times occurred in the Thousand
Islands of Lake Ontario, when our first-born was only a
couple of months old. My parents had joined us on this
particular trip, probably to satisfy themselves that their
only grandchild was not at risk. Unfortunately, the storm
that came up quickly that summer day was one of the
worst we've encountered in our sailing experience and,
no doubt, confirmed their worst fears. I couldn't be inside
the cabin for more than a few minutes without feeling
nauseated, yet I didn't want to bring my baby out in the
storm. My mother took over. One of the strongest memories both my husband and I retain of that trip is of my
mother sitting on the cabin sole ("because it's the safest
place," she said), holding her sleeping granddaughter, rid-
ing out the storm, and not budging until we reached port.

As we approached the dock we were grateful to see a
dozen hands reaching for docking lines and helping prevent our pitching boat from smashing against the dock.
The sailors ashore who had experienced the same gale
took turns helping each new arrival into their berth.
When we had time to pay attention to the VHF we discov-
ered that we had just weathered a blow that other boats
had not taken as well. The gale had struck the Toronto to
Prince Edward Island sailing fleet, racing to meet the Tall
Ships for their 1984 Quebec Rendezvous. We learned that
two sailboats had been dismasted and another two had
run aground. And the baby? She slept through it all.

●
The Good Times

Most people who start sailing with little ones continue, so the good times must outweigh the bad. In fact, some people are so positive about the experience that they have a hard time pinpointing the best time. "It was all good," they say.

One of the "best experiences" cited most often concerns the child's mastery of the sailing environment: watching sleeping baby bracing herself to adjust to the heel of the boat; sensing an infant's ease with the rough seas while the adults are unsure or afraid or feeling seasick; or having your children learn to row a dinghy before the age of four.

Eric Hatch beautifully captures this pride of accomplishment in describing his favorite moment. He brought along Hilary, his two-year-old daughter, for a day sail with adults with whom he was sailing for the first time:

There was enough breeze to move us well and heel us well over in the puffs. I looked down from the wind indicator to see Hilary climbing the companionway carrying a bag of chips. She stepped deftly into the cockpit, offered the chips around, then went back down the companionway, totally unconscious of the boat's movement, completely poised, and truly beautiful. It's worth the oatmeal strewn about the galley.

Other good moments come from families sharing together the joys of sailing: a broad reach, a sunny day, sitting at the bow with feet hanging over the edge and singing; watching the kids hanging upside down in the bosun's chair; greeting a family of dolphins traveling in the bow wave; being treated to a puppet show from behind the Vee-berth curtain. Anne Driver describes one of these moments:

The best time will always be a lovely memory: Sitting in the cockpit with my three babies while anchored off Petit

Bois Island, watching dolphins jump in the moonlit waters and stars twinkling above. The children all snuggled in and fell asleep. It was wonderful.

There is also something delightful in finding out that your time aboard has left a profound and positive impression on these little minds: watching the children play boat when they get home, hearing sailing vocabulary from a two-year-old mouth, listening to a four-year-old telling friends stories about your trip that even you have forgotten.

When I reflect back on sailing with our children, a kaleidoscope of wonderful memories floods my mind. One in particular sums it up for me: It is early August and our family is exploring Baie Fine in the North Channel of Lake Huron by dinghy. The sun has set and we are heading back to our sailboat anchored in beautiful Mary Anne Cove. The sky is darkening and the moon is bright in the sky; the trees are black silhouettes on the pink granite rock, glowing with green lichen patterns. I'm holding two-year-old Andrea in the bow of the little boat, and she throws out her arms and says, "Andy hug the moon. Andy hug the trees. Andy hug the rocks." In the eloquence of her limited vocabulary she captures for me why we're here. It is to feel that oneness with the land and the water, to sense our place in the universe, and ultimately to embrace life.

Those of you who sail with children already know of its joys. Those of you who are just starting out are in for a real treat. From time to time I do sail without my children, but I miss them. It just isn't the same.

appendix

contributors to
Babies Aboard

Pam Achurch
Snowgoose, Hughes 25
Penetanguishene, Ontario

Judy Button
Laser 28
Port Weller Marina,
St. Catherines, Ontario

Susan Cargo
Ericson 27
Idaho Falls, Idaho

Martin and Marie Cherry
Catalina 30
Oyster Bay, New York

Janis Couvreux
40-foot ketch
Melbourne, Florida

Anne Cudmore
Morgana, 36-foot ketch
Bowman, Dublin, Ireland

Ernie, Mel, Nicole, and
Evan Derushie
Wind's Will,
24-foot Stone Horse,
Hamilton, Ontario

Anne, David, Sally, Jefferson,
and Sam Driver
Sweetheart, Cal 2 - 27
Fort Worth, Texas

Ronald Dwelle, Jo Schneider,
Anna and Chase
Prudence P. Fishpaws,
Cheoy Lee Offshore 40
Newport, Rhode Island

Sydney and Sandra
Dumaresq
Surprise, C&C 38
Chester, Nova Scotia

Laura and David Estridge
Miracle, Baba 30
Seattle, Washington

Max Fletcher
Christopher Robin,
Westsail 32
Orr's Island, Maine

Lyndsay Green, Hank Intven,
Lauren and Andrea
Sweetwaters, CS 33
Toronto, Ontario

Sandra and Bruce Hansen
Whiskeyjack, Paceship 26
Northern Harbour, Manitoba

Eric Hatch
Catalina 25
Loveland, Ohio

Doris Hellenbart
Firewater, C&C 35
Windsor, Ontario

Sally and Bob Holden
Windago, 44-foot ketch
Vancouver, British Columbia

Dolly Hood
O'Day 25
Windsor, Maine

Nan, Kevin, Tristan, and
Colin Jeffrey
Kjersti, Heavenly Twins 26
catamaran
Portsmouth, New Hampshire

Margaret and Leo Litowich
Samurai, Irwin 38
Grand Rapids, Michigan

Gail and Alan Littlewood
Aquila, C&C 40
Toronto, Ontario

Lynn and Peter MacDonald
Moonfleet III, C&C 29
Pictou, Nova Scotia

Liz McCaughey
White Spirit, Northern 37
Cobourg, Ontario

Daniel Nichols
Silver Spring, Maryland

Sheila Rankin
Mariah, Tanzer 22
Port Credit, Ontario

Barbara and Roland Ross
Santa Barbara, Tanzer 24
Toronto, Ontario

Stuart Rulka
The Mikado, Yamaha 33
Burnaby, British Columbia

Joy Rundell
Honeycomb
Crestline, California

Sarah Smith
Courier, Cape Dory 36
Ft. Lauderdale, Florida

Larry and Dianna Snow
Aquilo, Hughes 29
Toronto, Ontario

Paul and Linda Starner
Greensleeves, Nonsuch 26
Traverse City, Missouri

Patricia Street
Iolaire, 1905 yawl
Roadtown, Tortola,
British Virgin Islands

Anne Taylor
Ottawa, Ontario

George and Kathleen Thirsk
Spontaneous, Aloha 34
Plymouth, Massachusetts

Sue, John, and Hannah
Viano
Mudlark, 60-foot schooner
Sandy Point, Maine

Anita Walter
35-foot sloop
Stamps Landing, Vancouver,
British Columbia

Irene Whitney
Darwin Sound II, Ocean 71
ketch
Sandspit, British Columbia

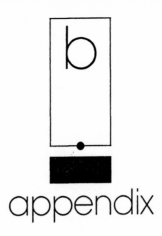

appendix

baby's packing list

clothing
- [ ] sleepers/pajamas
- [ ] undershirts
- [ ] tops and bottoms
- [ ] sweaters
- [ ] booties
- [ ] diapers
- [ ] plastic pants
- [ ] raincover
- [ ] sun hats
- [ ] knitted hats

comfort
- [ ] pacifiers
- [ ] snuggle sheet
- [ ] stuffed animal

play
- [ ] toys
- [ ] books
- [ ] animals/dolls
- [ ] audio tapes
- [ ] tape recorder

general gear
- [ ] life jacket
- [ ] sailing harness
- [ ] car seat/portable seat (mealtimes/playtimes)
- [ ] portable bed (sleeping structure)
- [ ] portable pool
- [ ] carrier
- [ ] small knapsack for on shore

- [ ] baby bedding: sheets and blankets (or sleeping bag)
- [ ] receiving blankets
- [ ] baby towels
- [ ] facecloths
- [ ] baby bottles and emergency supply of formula
- [ ] prepared baby food
- [ ] baby spoons and dishes
- [ ] baby manicure scissors
- [ ] baby hairbrush
- [ ] bibs
- [ ] changing mat
- [ ] diaper bag (or use small knapsack with changing mat)
- [ ] night-light and spare bulb
- [ ] batteries for tape recorder
- [ ] mosquito netting
- [ ] stroller
- [ ] sun parasol
- [ ] child care reference books

medical

(The following suggestions cover the basics only. Consult your doctor.)

- [ ] sunscreen
- [ ] mosquito repellant
- [ ] calamine lotion
- [ ] lip gloss with sunscreen
- [ ] vitamins
- [ ] petroleum jelly
- [ ] diaper rash cream
- [ ] thermometer
- [ ] baby wipes
- [ ] medication to reduce fever
- [ ] antiseptic cream
- [ ] bandages
- [ ] cotton swabs
- [ ] baby soap (body)
- [ ] baby shampoo
- [ ] laundry soap (not detergent)
- [ ] ipecac syrup
- [ ] first-aid kit

toddler's packing list

clothing

- [ ] shorts
- [ ] tee-shirts
- [ ] long pants
- [ ] long-sleeved shirts
- [ ] sweaters
- [ ] sleepers/pajamas
- [ ] bathing suit
- [ ] running shoes (shore shoes and boat shoes)
- [ ] plastic shoes (beach shoes)
- [ ] socks
- [ ] diapers/underpants
- [ ] raingear
- [ ] rain boots
- [ ] sunglasses
- [ ] hats (2)

comfort

- [ ] pacifiers
- [ ] snuggle sheet
- [ ] stuffed animal

play

- [ ] toys
- [ ] specially put together toys such as a toy tackle box for "tools"
- [ ] books
- [ ] tools for drawing, painting, constructing, etc.
- [ ] animals/dolls

- [ ] audio tapes
- [ ] tape recorder

general gear

- [ ] life jacket
- [ ] sailing harness
- [ ] portable seat (mealtimes)
- [ ] portable pool
- [ ] fishing gear
- [ ] backpack
- [ ] small knapsack for on shore
- [ ] bedding: sheets and blankets (or sleeping bag)
- [ ] towels: bathroom
- [ ] towels: bathing
- [ ] facecloths
- [ ] children's cutlery
- [ ] drinking straws
- [ ] children's sunglasses
- [ ] bibs
- [ ] batteries for tape recorder
- [ ] mosquito netting
- [ ] party supplies
- [ ] electric outlet covers
- [ ] potty seat cover (if needed)
- [ ] stroller (if needed)
- [ ] beach parasol
- [ ] child care reference books

medical

(The following suggestions cover the basics only; consult your doctor.)

☐ sunscreen
☐ mosquito repellant
☐ calamine lotion
☐ lip gloss with sunscreen
☐ vitamins
☐ petroleum jelly
☐ diaper rash cream
☐ thermometer
☐ wipes
☐ medication to reduce fever
☐ antiseptic cream
☐ bandages
☐ cotton swabs
☐ soap
☐ shampoo
☐ toothbrush
☐ toothpaste
☐ ipecac syrup
☐ first-aid kit

bibliography

recommended reference books

health and safety

American Medical Association. *The AMA Handbook of First Aid and Emergency Care.* New York: Random House, 1980.
A comprehensive guide to first aid and emergency medicine, covering everything from broken bones and burns to heart attacks, shock, and emergency childbirth.

Politano, Colleen, and Joan Neudecker. *Adrift: Boating Safety for Children.* Sidney, British Columbia: Porthole Press Ltd., 1986.
A story that teaches boating safety and seamanship about two children adrift in a dinghy. Although aimed at children between the ages of 8 and 12, it is also written for parents.

Seah, Stanley S. K., M.D., Ph.D. *Don't Drink the Water: The Complete Traveller's Guide to Staying Healthy in Warm Climates,* Toronto: Grosvenor Travel Series Book, co-published with the Canadian Public Health Association, 1983.
This book includes the dos and don'ts of eating, drinking, swimming, heat exhaustion, etc., that should be followed to ensure illness-free travel in warm climates. It lists the essentials for assembling a tropical medicine kit, and includes a section on childhood diseases.

Spock, Benjamin M. and Michael B. Rothenburg. *Dr. Spock's Baby and Child Care*. New York: Pocket Books, 1976.
The best all-around book on baby and child care, this guide has been revised to keep it up-to-date. Dutton also publishes an illustrated fortieth anniversary edition.

Whitehead, Lana E., and Lindsay R. Curtis, M.D. *How to Watersafe Infants and Toddlers*. Tuscon, Arizona: HP Books, 1983.
A step-by-step program for teaching your infant or toddler water safety and water fun. (Out of print.)

traveling with children

Brown, Tom, Jr. and Brandt Morgan. *Tom Brown's Field Guide to Nature and Survival for Children*. New York: Berkley Publishing Group, 1989.
A book to help you discover the wonders of nature with children—safely. Written by an outdoorsman and naturalist, this book shows how to make your trip, whether a day trip to a local park or a long wilderness trek, a safe and educational wilderness adventure.

Doan, Marlyn. *Starting Small in the Wilderness: The Sierra Club Outdoors Guide for Families*. San Francisco: Sierra Club Books, 1979.
A parent's guide to family camping activities, including day hiking, tent and car camping, backpacking, canoeing and kayaking, bicycling, snowshoeing, and cross-country skiing. Includes games and amusements, establishing camp rules, safety and first aid, and the joys of discovering the natural world. Also has instructions for making children's gear, such as rain pants.

Euser, Barbara J. *Take 'em Along: Sharing the Wilderness with Your Children*. Evergreen, Colorado: Cordillera Press, 1987.
This book encourages people to share the wilderness with their children, and includes sections on hiking, backpacking, cross-country skiing, horse packing, canoeing, and bicycling.

Hagstrom, Julie. *Travelling Games for Babies*. New York: Pocket Books, 1981.
Travelling games to play with young children from newborn to five years of age.

Lansky, Vicki. *Traveling with Your Baby*. New York: Bantam Books, 1985.
Practical tips on travelling with infants or small children, including planning, packing, and travelling by car, plane, train, or bus.

Losos, Dr. Joe, Dr. Alistair Clayton, Nancy Gerein, and Ruth Wilson. *Children Abroad: A Guide For Families Travelling Overseas.* Toronto: Deneau Publishers, 1986.
A guide to health and safety for families travelling overseas for extended periods, including health preparation, schooling, legal and financial arrangements, safety, illness, medical needs, and coming home.

Pentes, Tina, and Adrienne Truelove. *Travelling with Children to Indonesia & South-East Asia.* Sydney, NSW, Australia: Hale & Iremonger, 1984.
How to travel with children safely, cheaply, and happily to Indonesia and South-East Asia. Includes information on costs, accommodation suitable for families, tips on local customs, a medical section, and a section on learning the language.

Wheeler, Maureen. *Travel with Children: A Survival Kit For Travel in Asia,* Berkeley: Lonely Planet Publications, 1985.
Advice on traveling with children in Asia, including how to prepare yourself and your child for travel, what to take, and what to watch out for.

general recommendations

Travel with Your Children (TWYCH), 80 Eighth Avenue, New York, NY, USA, 10011.
TWYCH is a resource information center providing detailed information on family holidays worldwide. It publishes a regular newsletter, among other publications.

International Association for Medical Assistance to Travellers (IAMAT) 40 Regal Rd., Guelph, Ontario, Canada N1K 1B5.

cruising with children

books

Churchill, J. M., and P.A. Station. *Crafts & Games for Cruising Kids.* Toronto: Seacraft Publications, 1983.
Crafts and games for cruising children between the ages of three and seven. Designed to encourage imaginative use of ordinary materials usually found on board, combined with basic tools such as scissors, Magic Markers, and glue. Includes patterns.

Cornell, Gwenda. *Cruising With Children*. London: Adlard Coles Limited, 1986.
Practical advice on the many problems that coastal or deep-sea cruising parents may encounter with children of all ages. Half of the book is devoted to education afloat for school-age children. (This book is available through International Marine Publishing Company.)

Driscoll, Pippa. *Children Afloat*. Hove, East Sussex, England: Fernhurst Books, 1989.
A general discussion of sailing with children with some references to babies. Includes sections on how to provision and cook for the family at sea, recovering a man overboard, sending a Mayday call, and using flares. The book is based on the author's experiences cruising with children in a wide variety of boats and sea conditions. (This book is available through International Marine Publishing Company.)

magazine articles

Barnsley, Pam. "Safety For Your Waterbabies." *Pacific Yachting*, September 1981.

Barnsley, Pam. "Tips For Cruising With Kids." *Cruising World*, June 1983.

Bowyer, Elizabeth. "Boating With A Baby." *Great Expectations*, April 1983.

Bretz, Jay. "Children at Sea." *Pacific Yachting*, July 1986.

Erwin, Virgil. "Hand, Reef and Diaper." *Cruising World*, September 1982.

Sweetland, Jane. "Cruising with VSP's (Very Small Persons)." *Waterfront*, July 1986.

recommended books for preschoolers

Armitage, Ronda and David. *The Lighthouse Keeper's Catastrophe*. London: Puffin Books, 1988.
The lighthouse keeper accidently locks the key in the lighthouse and must take desperate measures to put the light on before a storm endangers lives. A tale of true bravery that helps explain the function and importance of the lighthouse.

Baker, Jeannie. *Where the Forest Meets the Sea.* New York: Greenwillow Books, 1987.
This remarkable book begins with the sentence, "My father knows a place we can only reach by boat," and goes on to vividly portray the magic of discovering and exploring the wilderness. The extraordinary images are created through life-like collages and beautifully support the message: a plea for those areas of the world that are in danger of extinction.

Blades, Ann. *By the Sea: An Alphabet Book.* Toronto: Kids Can Press, 1985.
An alphabet book beautifully illustrated with things found near the sea.

Brown, M. K. *Let's Go Swimming with Mr. Sillypants.* New York: Crown Publishers, 1986.
Mr. Sillypants lives by the ocean, but he has never learned to swim. One day he decides to take the plunge and sign up for swimming lessons, but his fears start to get the better of him. This very funny book conveys the idea that water is a place where even a sillypants can feel at home.

Burningham, John. *Mr. Gumpy's Outing.* Harmondsworth, England: Puffin Books, 1970.
This book is not about a sailboat or the sea; it's about a river-boat. A delightful story of what happens when you try to get everybody into the same boat.

Carruth, Jane. *Tiggy and the Giant Wave.* New York: Modern Promotions/Publishers, 1984.
Tiggy goes to the seashore to visit Uncle Pintog the sailor, and gets knocked over by a big wave. By the end of the book she has mastered her fear of the water. This is a good book to help you talk to your children about these kinds of accidents and their fears. (Out of print.)

Dawe, Karen. *Beach Book and Beach Bucket.* New York: Workman Publishing, 1988.
A seashore companion for young beachcombers, complete with a bucket with a punctured top, this book includes a seashell collector's guide, tips on safe beach exploration, information on how to identify each discovery, and suggests many imaginative beach projects. The book is recommended for ages 10 and under. Although too advanced for preschoolers on their own, it is perfect with adult assistance.

Delgado, Eduard, and Francesca Rovira. *Alex's Adventures at the Harbor.* New York: Derrydale Books, 1986.
During Alex's visit to the harbor, a freighter and passenger ship collide, dumping the freighter's crew and load of zoo an-

imals into the water. While the rescue is underway, a fishing boat begins to sink under its heavy load of fish. The illustrations are full of detail, and many of the characters can be followed from page to page as their own separate adventures unfold. Games related to the story make up the last pages of the book. (Out of print.)

Dupasquier, Philippe. *The Harbour*. London: Walker Books, 1984.
This account of a day at the harbor includes fishing boats departing and returning with their catch, a sailboat going for a sail, and the unsuccessful launching of a cabin cruiser.

Field, Eugene. *Wynken, Blynken, and Nod*. New York: E.P. Dutton, 1982.
This tale of a magical moonlight sail in a wooden shoe is a beloved bedtime poem of childhood. A number of versions of the poem are available, but Susan Jeffers' illustrations are particularly enchanting. An excellent "good night" book.

Fowler, Richard. *Mr. Little's Noisy Boat*. Toronto: Thomas Allen & Son, 1987.
A "lift-the-flap" book that builds boating vocabulary, including words such as "cotter pin" and "propeller shaft." This is an engaging story about Mr. Little trying to track down the source of sounds on his boat. Terrific for training little ones' ears to listen to and recognize the sounds around them, and not a bad vocabulary exercise for adults either. A delightful combination of play and learning.

Haas, Irene. *The Maggie B*. New York: Aladdin Books, Macmillan Co., 1984.
A little girl's wish to sail for a day on a boat named after her "with someone nice for company" comes true. Sailing families will appreciate the sentiment that the "someone nice" is her brother James, who is "a dear baby." This charming book, with lovely illustrations, is particularly good at conveying how snug and warm it can be in a boat during a storm.

Hayward, Linda. *Sail Away! A Phonic Reader with Learning Cards*. New York: Random House, Learning Ladders Series, 1988.
A first reader and learning card kit for children through six years of age. The book has bright pictures of two rabbit friends going out for a race in their dinghy, and shows familiar sailing scenes, including leaving a marina, bringing in fenders, untying lines, hoisting sails, etc. There are some especially nice racing scenes, with pictures of the little boats heeling and the spray splashing the sailors. The learning cards have few sailing images but lots of play potential.

Heller, Nicholas. *An Adventure at Sea.* New York: Greenwillow Books, 1988.
Older brother Harold takes his brother and sister on a trip through the world of his imagination, turning the old cardboard box in the backyard into a tall-masted ship and Henry the dog into a terrifying sea monster. This book humorously recreates childhood play by juxtaposing the actual backyard scene on one page with the imaginary one on the other.

Hill, Eric. *S. S. Happiness Crew Book of Numbers.* San Francisco: Determined Productions, 1983.
A learn-to-count, "lift-the-flap" book based on life aboard the *S.S. Happiness.* Items used for counting include life preservers, knots, and buoys. (Out of print.)

Jonas, Ann. *Reflections.* New York: Greenwillow Books, 1987.
This book is for everyone who has sat with a child, staring at refections in the water and imagining whole worlds. It recreates a child's perfect day, beginning with the sentence, "The best place I know is here by the sea." In each full-color picture another picture is reflected; the water scenes are particularly beautiful.

Kellogg, Steven. *The Island of the Skog.* New York: The Dial Press, 1973.
A group of mice set sail in search of a peaceful island, read the compass backward, end up among icebergs, and land on an island inhabited by a skog. Through fear and lack of communication, mice and skog each try to rid the island of the other. The story ends happily with an agreement to live together as friends. When our elder daughter was two and a half this was one of her favorites. It has just the right level of scariness combined with a happy ending.

Lear, Edward. *The Owl and the Pussycat.* New York: Scholastic Book Services, 1984.
Edward Lear's classic poem is imaginatively illustrated by Ron Berg in this tale of the owl and the pussycat who go off to sea in a beautiful pea-green boat.

Levinson, Riki. *Our Home is the Sea.* New York: E. P. Dutton, 1988.
A Chinese boy hurries home from school to his family's houseboat in Hong Kong Harbor. It is the end of the school year, and he is anxious to join his father and grandfather in fishing, their family profession. This book is illustrated with oil paintings of Hong Kong, of both downtown and harbor life. It is a wonderful way to help children imagine other cultures and ways of life on the sea.

Lionni, Leo. *Fish Is Fish*. New York: Alfred A. Knopf, 1987.
When a tadpole grows into a frog and tries to tell his fish friend back in the pond what the big wide world is like, the fish's imagination runs wild. This book's illustrations are both enchanting and hilarious and can stimulate children to think creatively about the new worlds around them.

Lionni, Leo. *Swimmy*. New York: Alfred A. Knopf, 1987.
When his school of fish is swallowed by a tuna, Swimmy is the sole survivor. He devises an ingenious plan to camouflage himself and his new companions. This exquisite, award-winning picture book will help your children visualize the world beneath the sea.

Locker, Thomas. *Sailing with the Wind*. New York: Dial Books, 1986.
As Elizabeth travels in Uncle Jack's small sailboat down the river from her house to the ocean she has never seen, land and water and sky change constantly. By the time Elizabeth returns home she has had a taste of the splendor and mystery of the wider world, and you will too after reading this book. Each picture is a full-color reproduction of an oil painting. This is an exquisite and eloquent book.

Maestro, Betsy, and Ellen DelVecchio. *Big City Port*. New York: Scholastic Book Services, 1984.
A book that illustrates with clear pictures and simple words the various activities that take place in a big-city port.

Mahy, Margaret. *The Man Whose Mother Was a Pirate*. New York: Viking Penguin, Inc. 1986.
This is a delightful story of a pirate mother who drags her son away from his drab office back to the sea, where they become crew on Sailor Sam's ship. Both the words and the illustrations of this book eloquently portray the wonderful allure of the sea.

Patrick, Denice. *Look Inside a Ship*. New York: Grosset & Dunlap, The Putnam Publishing Group, A Poke & Look Learning Book, 1989.
This "Poke & Look Learning Book," made of heavy board pages filled with die-cut holes to poke and peek through, allows one to explore what goes on inside a ship. It is designed to show preschoolers how ships work, who sails on board, and what ships carry to faraway lands. This book allows children to visualize what the freighters they see look like inside. References to other ships are included.

Peppe, Rodney. *The Kettleship Pirates*. Harmondsworth, England: Kestrel Books, 1983.

An old kettleship turns into a pirate ship, sets off to search for buried treasure, and returns home safe and sound. The different levels of dialogue and meaning in this book make it suitable for a broad range of ages.

Rogers, Paul. *Forget-Me-Not.* New York: Penguin Books, Inc., 1986.
Sydney the forgetful lion visits Cousin Joe, who lives in a lighthouse, then promptly starts losing things. Young children will enjoy figuring out what Sidney has lost and pointing out where he left it.

Sendak, Maurice. *Where the Wild Things Are.* New York: Harper & Row, 1963.
In this award-winning book Max is sent to his room and, through his imagination, escapes on a sailboat to the land of the wild things. This book is not about sailing per se. Rather, it is about how a sailboat can transport you into other worlds at those times when you most need to escape.

Thompson, Richard. *Effie's Bath.* Toronto: Annick Press, 1989.
Effie and her playmate dive to the bottom of the bathtub and are transported to the sea. There they are rescued by the owl and the pussycat (in their beautiful pea-green boat) and help organize their marriage—complete with Piggy-wig and runcible spoon—until circumstances return them to their bathtub. This book is great fun, particularly for children familiar with the Edward Lear poem, who will find themselves transported into the story.

Thompson, Richard. *Gurgle, Bubble, Splash.* Toronto: Annick Press, 1989.
When Jesse goes for a holiday at the seaside she doesn't like the sea at first. Soon she grows to love it, however, and misses it terribly when she returns home. One day the sea arrives in a box in the mail and causes a terrible mess, but Jesse convinces the ocean to return home if she promises to visit again. Delightful text and illustrations and a great book for back home again.

Transport Parade Series. *At Sea.* Newmarket, Suffolk, England: Brimax Books, 1982.
A colorful board book with illustrations and simple descriptions of different types of boats.

Turnbull, Ann. *The Sand Horse.* Toronto: McClelland & Stewart, 1989.
This haunting book about freedom and the sea is based on the story of an artist and his creation, a horse sculpted in sand. When the tide rushes in the sand horse springs to life and

joins the "white horses"—the white caps—in the sea. The watercolor illustrations exquisitely capture the beauty of the ocean in its many moods.

Wernhard, Hermann. *What Can You See On the Water?* London: Methuen Children's Books, 1983.
A board book without words and with vivid, simple pictures of things you can see on or in the water. Sturdy, colorful, and a good vocabulary builder.

Brown, Margaret Wise. *The Sailor Dog.* Racine, Wisconsin: Western Publishing Company, 1953.
Scuppers the sailor dog, who was "born at sea in the teeth of a gale," tries farm life but is lured back to sea. He is shipwrecked, ends up in a seaport in a foreign land, and always manages to get back to his ship. Children will identify with the words and pictures about Scuppers' "little room" down below, where everything is hung up in its right place and Scuppers sleeps snuggly in his bunk.

Wynne-Jones, Tim. *Zoom at Sea.* Topsfield, Massachusetts: Salem House Publications, 1986.
Zoom, a water-loving cat, discovers a map to the sea, follows its directions, and goes on a fantastic sea adventure. This book is a wonderfully lyrical rendering of the magic of the sea.

Ziefert, Harriet. *My Sister Says Nothing Ever Happens When We Go Sailing.* New York: Harper & Row, 1986.
The family goes for a sail but sister doesn't want to be along. When the wind dies down she falls asleep and misses all the action, including a rain squall and a rescue at sea. She wakes up when the boat docks. As the story unfolds, so does the book, into a colorful frieze that provides a map to everything sister has missed.

general recommendation

Annikins Books by Annick Press of Toronto.
These are small (3½ by 3½ inch) versions of regular size and length books and are perfect for boating or traveling in general.

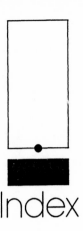

Index